GOOD COP

GIRL COP

The Secret Life of a Police Officer
What you always wanted to know
about policing but were afraid to ask

LISA DOBLE

DEDICATION

This book is dedicated to my
loving husband Jason, and our three sons;
Jack, Thomas and Joseph who always
support me in my crazy ideas.

This book is also dedicated to my
mom Dianne, dad Kevin and brother David
who were there for me,
when I chose to be a cop.

***GRAB YOUR FREE GIFT ***

"25 LIFE LESSONS LEARNED FROM LAW ENFORCEMENT"

Download your Inspirational Poster and Life Lessons 100% FREE:

https://mailchi.mp/4494387e551f/25-life-lessons-learned-from-law-enforcement-free

** WARNING **

This book contains very coarse language,
some sexual content, real life stories and
examples of police work, that some people
may find offensive or disturbing.

It is *not* intended to be for shock value,
but for educational purposes.
Reader discretion is advised.

TABLE OF CONTENTS

Introduction   9

1 How it all began   15

2 All in a day's work   29

3 Human misbehavior   43

4 Death becomes everyone   59

5 What it takes to wear the badge   75

6 The "other" F word: Female   89

7 Myths, misconceptions and common
   questions   105

8 Evidence and crime scenes   119

9 The good, the bad and the boring   137

10 Life lessons learned from law
   enforcement   151

Acknowledgments   163

About the Author   167

INTRODUCTION

Your daughter, son, sister or maybe you have always wanted to be a cop. You or a loved one have wondered about it, pondered it, agonized over it, or are simply intrigued by it. You know you just want to make a difference in the world, but can you be truly prepared for what's to come?

You've sat and watched your favorite crime shows on TV, and read crime novels—but not everything is fit for TV viewing. Believe me. Maybe you or someone you know is rethinking the decision to join (or not join) the force.

And as much as we think we know what goes on in the world, human nature will never cease to surprise. This book is a true and correct excerpt of my fifteen years on the front line, as a police officer in Australia. Just when I thought

I had heard, seen, and done it all, there were more shocking, gruesome, funny, and bizarre events at every turn.

If you have always wondered what it is really, truly like to be a cop, then wonder no more. This book will tell it like it is; no bullshit, no exaggeration, and nothing is off limits. If you are unclear about joining the force or have someone in your life that is unsure about taking that step, then this book will be a realistic snapshot of what to expect. It is not watered down, it is not sugar-coated—just plain and simple truth.

This book is not intended just for shock value, it is intended to be an honest eye-opener to help you decide if policing is a career for you or your significant others. Even if you have no intention of being a cop and never have, this book will give you valuable insight into the world of human beings at their worst, so you may be better informed and able to stay safe in your own life.

The examples, opinions, and stories contained within are from my personal experience and point of view. Because I was a police officer for fifteen years, I learned some valuable life lessons myself. I have now passed these lessons on to my own children—like keeping safe and knowing your surroundings—being slightly suspicious of everyone, and not taking things at face value.

I told my boys this simply to open their eyes and see people and situations for what they are. Understanding the truth about crime and human nature is something that is now second nature to me, and I carry those skills with me today, long after leaving the force.

With crime in the community at an all-time high, my experience can help you understand the types of things cops face, and the dangers out there. It will help you understand what police go through, why a loved one may be considering the force and what might attract them to it.

My career has given me some valuable insight into human nature and helped me to be confident, strong, and feel capable enough to take care of myself. But you don't need to become a cop to gain an understanding of what took me fifteen years to find out. This book will educate you, entertain you, and open your eyes and mind.

This book is essentially me on a page—it is easy to read and will have you drawing on my experience in no time. The last chapter has 25 life lessons that I learned from being a cop, that you can implement into your life today. If you get nothing else out of this book, I guarantee you will see people and situations differently.

You don't want to end up a statistic or be one of the feature stories on the crime channel. Don't be the person who believes everything people say and doesn't think there are dangerous people out there. Don't be the person who has no concept of the criminal mind and is oblivious to evil.

Be the person who is one step ahead of the game. Allow this book to help you challenge things when they don't seem quite right and open your mind to see the full picture. Knowledge is power, and you never know when you might need to call upon that power. And my promise to you is to tell the raw, and honest truth.

The book you are about to read will take you on a wild, eye opening ride. You might even feel like you are right there in the patrol car with me. You may be shocked, horrified, grossed out, or saddened at times, as what you are about to read is not for the faint of heart.

Does it have absolutely *everything* I know in it? Well, no, of course not. There are some things I can't or shouldn't write about, and some things I won't write about out of respect for the people involved. Some things are best left unsaid. Hey, I am not a monster.

What you are about to read is touching, funny, disgusting, unbelievable, shocking and at times bizarre. What you are about to read is in your face, and a serious word of warning..... I curse like a trucker, so if you are opposed to R-rated bad language and factual (but somewhat disturbing) tales, then maybe this is *not* the book for you.

For everyone else, let's kick ass.

CHAPTER ONE

How It All Began

You know when you were a kid and other kids would say things like "When I grow up I want to be a fireman, or a doctor, or a teacher"? Well I never said that. I didn't say much about what I wanted to be when I grew up because I didn't know. All I did know was that I couldn't wait to leave school, and I was not going to college.

At the time, in Australia, people only went to college if they wanted to pursue professions like medicine, accounting, or education. I felt I had no reason to go at that time, so work was the best option for me. So, I left school at fifteen, and took my first job in a bank.

It wasn't what I *wanted* but it was better than school. I was bored to death with that shit. But I still didn't have a clue about what I did want to do long term. Unlike my husband, who says from the time he can remember, all he ever wanted to be was a policeman, but I will come back to him in a later chapter.

What I am about to share is how I took a lame suggestion from a couple of co-workers, and made a life-changing decision at a very young age. This decision had a profound impact on my life, and made me the person I am today. This also allowed me to follow my dream regardless of how others felt about it. This was *my* life, fuck everyone else and their opinion.

Bank Blues

Back in the mid-1980s, the bank was a good stable job, but it was just a job. I knew that eventually I would want, and need, more than opening bank accounts and handing out money. But it was not until two work colleagues left the bank, and joined the police force that I started to think about what else I could do.

One day, they both came in with their uniforms on, telling me how great the force was, and that I should consider it myself. I distinctly remember laughing at the pair of them, and saying, "I could never do that." But after some more words of encouragement, I walked away thinking that it *might* be a career for me.

One option was to stay there filling out deposit slips and counting cash, and keep doing the same thing day in day out, or I could do something different—something that had some meaning. I remember looking over at my boss sitting in his glass cubicle, right in the middle of the office. He was a sleazy bastard, but somewhat helpful, as he had been in the bank for a long time.

As usual, he had his feet up on the desk, talking on the phone, smoking a cigarette and reading a black label edition of a porno magazine. For years, he had the magazine sent to the office so that his wife never found out he had a subscription. I stared at him, subconsciously shaking my head, and at that point, my decision made *me*—I didn't make *it*.

So, after years of wandering aimlessly in the bank, I finally had a real goal: to join the New South Wales Police Force.

New Beginnings

My next step was to tell my family and friends about my new career path. I thought I would be prepared for all the various reactions I would get. I had made my decision to join the force on the Friday after my conversation with my two ex-colleagues. All weekend I was thinking of ways to tell my family, and I had a response ready for each reaction they might have had.

I remember telling my mom, dad, and brother over a Sunday night dinner. I didn't use any pre-prepared script, I just blurted out, "I am going to join the police force." Of course, my family thought it was a great idea, and they could see me being a cop.

Well, that's a relief. I knew they would be supportive as always, but I had just made a pretty big statement, and nobody in my family had ever done anything like that. As I went on to tell friends, and people that I knew, the negative comments started to come out. But I didn't give a fuck, I was excited about it and committed to seeing it through.

Some supported me, some questioned my choice, and others just plain criticized it. I guess this is a pretty standard response. I got the speech from a few workmates about how dangerous the job would be, and that it is not the place for women to work. Well, saying that to me is like waving a red rag at a bull.

Sure, the bank had been a great job to start in, but I only really did it because I didn't have another goal in mind, and my mom had started working in the bank at a young age also. At that point, I didn't care what anybody thought about it, I was joining, it was a done deal. Like it or don't.

After I joined, there was one question that was commonly asked of me by everybody, whether they liked my decision or not. That question was, "Why did you join?" I had no magical answer for that. It was not a lifelong dream. I was not on a crusade to save the world from evil. I didn't even really do it because I had a burning desire to help people.

That last one is a common reason for joining the force. The basic truth is that it literally seemed like a good idea at the time. I had the shits with the bank, I was sick of my weasel boss, and found myself asking if this was as good as it gets. So without trying to sound too much like a smartass, when I was asked that question, the answer was plain and simple..... I joined because I wanted to.

Academy Life

Now, I won't bore you with all the details of the tests I took to get in, suffice to say there were numerous physical and psychological examinations, strength, agility, and aptitude tests. It was April 1989, I was twenty years old, and I was on my way to starting at the police academy, which was about six hours away from home. I remember my mom and I driving down there together, to the place I would call home for the next six months.

It was a Sunday. I got settled into my room. We were shown around the academy, and then it was time for me to drop my mom at the train station for her return trip. As she got on the train and it pulled away from the station, I turned to walk away with a sick feeling in my stomach and I said to myself, "What the fuck have I done?" I wanted to run after that train and go home, but I snapped out of it and reminded myself that I chose to do this.

It was a rude shock to the system. I was a small-town girl who wanted excitement from life, and I knew this was not going to disappoint. I was given Room 94 at the top of the stairwell on the third floor, which was more like a prison cell with carpet. It had a narrow single bed, a closet, a desk, and not much else.

I can't complain. It did have a nice view of the carpark, the water tanks, and the highway off in the distance. We started classes the next day, and I got a taste for what was coming. I had a stack of textbooks that were taller than me. I loved the speech all the new recruits got, especially when we were told that student officers were lower in rank than a police dog.

I was running many miles a day to keep up my level of fitness, and was living off cafeteria food. Oh, and I forgot to mention, that I was one of four girls in my class. I knew it was a male-dominated job, but four girls in my group? There were about ten classes within our intake, and some smaller groups only had two girls in them, so I considered myself lucky.

So just like in the movies, each person gets given a nickname by their classmates. We had all the usual suspects like Chicken Man, Smurf, Chuck, Doc and many more creative monikers. The nicknames generally came about due to a person's surname, something stupid they have done, or a personality trait.

Mine came about during a class of arm bar takedowns and leg sweeps. Smurf was a rather large guy, who got paired with a girl that was tall, but very, very thin. She had dark hair, wore it bundled up on top of her head and looked like Olive Oyl out of Popeye. So, class began and they were paired up first to try the leg sweep.

Personally, it is one my favorite moves, whereby you place your hand or forearm on a person's chest and push back, whilst simultaneously wrapping your leg around behind theirs and scooping the legs forward. You get the picture, and when combined with the element of surprise, it is a very effective move for getting a person on the ground, regardless of how big they are. The only problem here, Smurf was very big and Olive was totally not.

Smurf leg-swept Olive and drove her into the mats. She was winded, whilst he was showboating and laughing. Such a dick move, I was pissed. The instructor dismissed poor Olive

Oyl from the mat and asked for a volunteer to leg-sweep Smurf. I don't know why, but I jumped up instantly before anyone else had a chance to answer, and said "I'll do it" without a second thought.

It was only the first few days of training, so at this point I didn't have my nickname yet and nobody really knew each other. I walked onto the mat, watching Olive still gasping for air in the corner, and was told what to do by the instructor. When he said, "go," I did. And hard. Like, no mercy hard. I slammed that smiling prick into the mat as hard as I could.

Everybody cheered for me. He looked at the instructor and started to complain about how hard I had gone in on him. The instructor quickly reminded him that he had just had his turn, and that the people on the street won't give a fuck how hard they slam you. From that moment on, I was called "Lethal." I liked it, it didn't suck, it suited my personality, so I went with it.

First Station

Six months later, after many exams, and the walls of my room being covered in cardboard posters with powers of arrest and other points of law, I graduated the academy. It was a great day. But I knew the real work was about to begin, and I was posted to the inner city of Sydney. I was excited, scared, and doubting myself all at the same time, but all the "real" officers at the station were welcoming.

Along with their welcome wishes and well-meaning advice came another stupid question: "Where do you want to be in five years?" My answer to that, "I don't know, I just got here. Ask me again in five years." And, what was that sage advice from the real cops? Well, the first thing that came out of all the other officer's mouths was "Forget everything you learned at the academy."

Yeah, nice one. I just spent six months learning everything at the academy and now you're fucking telling me to forget it? What they meant was, the academy is good to learn the theory of policing, but it doesn't prepare you for the streets. That was the understatement of the year, as I would quickly come to learn.

I also quickly came to learn that cursing was a preferred language in the force. I mean, I used to curse a little bit, but after working with mostly men, spending my days amongst the criminal element, and being called every conceivable name you can imagine, I ended up cursing like a trucker. Still do.

At my first station I was also introduced to another famous phrase in our force. All the old dinosaurs that had been in the force forever—and were all bitter and twisted—would always say, "The job's fucked." I can't tell you how many times I heard this, which can be a bit disconcerting to somebody who has just achieved their dream of becoming a cop.

After being criticized by people for joining in the first place, I was now being criticized by the very people I work with. Problem was, although policing was an exciting career, that provided you a specific skill set, and some hard life lessons, officers at that time had no formal qualifications if they left. So, many officers felt as though they could not do anything else, as policing was all they knew. Hence the whining.

I didn't listen to that though, and nobody was going to talk me out of continuing as a cop. I had worked very hard to get to where I was, and decided not to let anybody try and bring me down, just because they were unhappy with their lives. Whenever someone would say "The job's fucked," I would respond, "then why don't you leave?"

And that was how it all began for me. I was working in a male-dominated field, on the mean streets of Sydney, and came to realize that the job was no joke. I didn't have a concept of how much I didn't know about life, until I came to the city and saw how the other half lives.

All this came about from my two old work-mates that told me that I would be good enough to be a cop too. That led me to follow my dreams, toward my new life-changing career. I had certainly been cocooned in my small lakeside hometown, and that was all about to change forever. Life got fucking hairy, very quickly, as you are about to find out.

CHAPTER TWO

All In a Day's Work

When things got tough at the academy, I had to keep reminding myself that I chose this. I put myself in this position. I decided that bank life was not enough for me and I decided to do something about it. The academy had its place, but what was to follow on the street later… wow, there's just no way you can learn that shit from a textbook.

In no time at all I would be knee deep in drugs, death, sex crimes, suicide, fist fights, siege situations, and car accidents. But before I get into all the juicy stuff, let's go back to where the academy left off and the "real" job came in.

Now Shit Gets Real

After spending six months eating hospital-type food and being told what to do, when, and how to do it, I was now at my first posting, which was an inner-city station in Sydney. Honestly, it was not that much different to the academy in that I was still being told what to do and when, minus the awful food. My first few shifts were a bit of a blur, but I distinctly remember my first night shift. It started at 11pm and finished at 7am.

Back then, we would do seven nights in a row and then get five days off. I turned up for my first night shift and was placed on station duty. I didn't mind as there was a lot to learn from inside as well as on the street, but it was such a quiet night that by 3am I couldn't stay awake. The duty officer came over to me, shook me to wake up, and told me to go home. I was no good to him in that condition.

My first station was huge, and very, very busy. I rapidly began having lots of firsts at that station. My first arrest, seeing my first body at the morgue, first death by AIDS, and my first autopsy. It did not take long for my eyes to be wide open. Just to go back, my first arrest was pretty cool.

First Arrest

It was a Saturday night, and I was unlucky enough to be partnered up with the big boss for the night. He was okay, and he was nice enough to me, but most people didn't like him because he was lazy and they called him Jabba the Hutt. About 7pm we got called to a restaurant, in a very busy entertainment precinct. There was a guy going crazy inside, and he had punched his girlfriend in front of everyone.

I was driving, and got out of the car to head inside and see what was going on. As I was walking up to the restaurant, I could see this huge monster of a guy—about 6'4"—throwing his arms around and pushing people into tables. *Oh shit, here we go.*

As I walked up to the restaurant, he started walking out the door, and I turned to say something to my partner, and fuck me....... the lazy old prick was still sitting in the car talking on the radio. Unfortunately, I was now on my own, an arm's length from this monster of a man, and about one week fresh out of the academy. I decided that I had to do something and fast, because based on what I had just seen inside, talking was not going to cut it.

Now, this is where that leg-sweep lesson I learned at the academy comes in. I stepped up to him, pushed him in the chest, and swept his legs out from under him before he knew what was happening. I fucking folded him up like a swiss army knife, then flipped him over and cuffed him, all by myself. Proud moment. Then I stood back and realized how wrong that could have gone.

By this time, Jabba had dragged his ass out of the car, as the guy was safely wrapped up in cuffs. We called for backup, and to my surprise, it took six officers to get him in the back of the police truck. *Holy shit.* Funny part was, he went to court, entered a guilty plea, and the judge forced him to write me a letter of apology. I gotta say, it was a harrowing, but fun experience.

First Death

Another first, that was anything but fun, was attending my first death. This was a middle-aged guy that lived with his partner in a very expensive part of town. This was the late 1980s so AIDS and HIV were still the great unknown, and a certain death sentence. Because the victim had been suffering from a life-threatening illness, his doctor happily wrote a death certificate and off he went to the funeral directors. No autopsy needed.

This is not that remarkable, nor exciting except that a few months ago, I was watching a true crime program on TV, and this case was the featured story. I called out to my husband, Jason, and told him that this was the first ever death case I had attended. I did not know it at the time, as I had gone to another station shortly after, but about twelve months after the man seemingly died from AIDS, his partner was murdered by their financial advisor over money.

Apparently, the family told authorities some time later, that they had suspicions about the death of the "AIDS" guy, and it turns out he was murdered too. They had hosted a dinner party the night before, which I remember had happened, and it seems the financial advisor helped the guy along with a pillow over his face.

First Morgue Visit

Even though the guy with AIDS was the first body I ever saw, he just looked like he was asleep in bed. Going to the city morgue was a whole other story. Being a new officer, I got dragged out there and shown around. I remember walking into this huge coolroom area, and there were rows and rows of metal fridge drawers. The place smelt like a fucking butcher's shop, it was disgusting and very creepy.

So, of course, my partner couldn't wait to open some of the drawers and show me what was inside. They too looked like they were asleep, to a degree, but there were people with parts missing, some had been beaten and had severe injuries, and some were kids. There was also a guy cut in half.

It was not a pleasant experience at all, but unfortunately, it's a huge part of the job. The sights I can handle, the smell not so much. It is a clinical, chemical smell combined with the smell of meat that gets up your nose, and in your clothes. My husband was a cop too, and I could always tell if he had been to the morgue. I could smell it.

First Drug Operation

Enough about that death stuff for now, as I have a whole chapter on it—being that it is a big part of being a cop. Police work is dangerous, diverse, and exciting. You will face different incidents every day. Minute by minute things change, and even if you have been to a hundred car accidents, stabbings or assaults, they are all different.

These jobs can be funny, bizarre, gruesome, heartbreaking, maddening, and senseless, sometimes all rolled into one, with plenty of "oh shit" moments. I remember working an undercover drug operation at a large rave party, where we were given money to buy ecstasy and then bust the dealers. At the end of the night we were out the front of the venue, and stopped a car to check the occupants.

They were a bit smart lipped but everything checked out fine. We kept working, and soon after, my partner gets a call that those same people had handed his police badge into a station. It seems when he leaned into the car, which is a big mistake, his badge fell out. Shocked, he turned to me and said, "Oh well, lucky it wasn't my fucking gun." Whoops.

Other Crazy Shit

Of course, not every job is that easy, and by the time I had spent a few years on the force I had run the gauntlet of police work. I had arrested one on the gladiators, from the TV show of the same name, for assaulting a guy. I had arrested a man that had gagged and tied his nine-year-old stepdaughter's arms and legs to her four-post bed, and anally raped her whilst her mother was in the next room.

I attended a stabbing where a woman was sliced open on the street, not far from the police station. Her ex-boyfriend was upset with her for breaking up with him, and he cut her from the chest to the navel at 3 o'clock in the afternoon. Her guts were hanging out all over the sidewalk.

I had attended a suicide where a guy was lying in bed on the phone to his estranged wife, and said "Listen to this, you fucking bitch" before shooting himself in the head. An electrician came in the next day to finish a job in the roof space, and thought the guy was just asleep in bed.

Then there was a domestic violence incident where the perpetrator was a woman. Her husband had a restraining order against her, so she wasn't supposed to be there. She came outside the home, with a newborn baby in one arm and a house brick in the other. We were worried that she was about to cave the kid's head in.

We cornered her in the back yard, and crash tackled her. I was punching her as hard as I could to make her let go of the baby. That bitch had a hard head and was happily taking my fists in her face. But we got the baby and tossed it over the fence to the other officers. She also got a mouthful of pepper spray for her trouble.

People just do some crazy shit. Another highlight was a siege situation where the tactical officers, all dressed in black, were trying to negotiate with some idiot, that had his wife and kids held hostage in his home. I got called to attend, and was not disappointed when I got put on the outer perimeter. I didn't feel like getting my fucking head blown off that day.

After a few hours of sitting in the patrol car, watching the scene from a distance, I got called to go down to the command post. I was far more experienced than the guy I was working with, so the boss wanted me to go. I got down to the command post, not knowing why I was there, and was told to go up into the house next door to the gunman, and be briefed by the tactical team.

What the fuck? You want me to go up there in a blue uniform, with no fancy equipment and my little Smith and Wesson six-shot revolver?

But the boss assured me it would be okay, they would give me a bulletproof vest. Well that's great, unless you get shot in the fucking head.

Anyway, off I went, crawling on my hands and knees, along a brick fence so he didn't see me. I was briefed of the situation by the tactical team, and positioned in the garage of the home next door to the scene, by myself. I could see the suspect pacing around the house, holding a large caliber rifle. The man had let his wife and child leave the house, and was now alone inside, threatening to kill himself or police.

The tactical guys went off to set their snipers in place, and told me as they were leaving, "If he comes your way, just shoot him and we will figure it out later." I was sweating bullets, trying to imagine how I would have a chance at stopping him with his large rifle, and me with my little revolver. Luckily it ended peacefully after ten hours, as the guy got tired and surrendered, but not before I spent all night in that garage.

Not all jobs are exciting or adrenaline-fuelled and some can be quite mundane, but when my days weren't filled with jobs like those I have mentioned, I was busy attending other crazy jobs. Motor vehicle accidents, bomb threats, bank robberies, major sporting events, protest rallies, riots, conducting search warrants, dismantling meth labs, and pulling marijuana crops, just to name a few.

Then there's attending dog complaints, neighborhood disputes, break-ins and assault and battery incidents. Dealing with mental health is also a massive part of the job, and you never know how people will react when they see the police. You get the picture. Every day is different.

Media Beat Up

All these wild happenings can sometimes attract media attention, especially if a crime involves a child, is particularly violent in nature, or involves a prominent person. The media can be your best friend or your worst nightmare. They have a way of reporting information that may not necessarily be true, but makes for a great headline.

Most cops have been splashed across the news channels or the papers, many times throughout their career, and the shots are not always flattering. Remember, we are dealing with the public when they are at their worst, so these are usually not pics for the family album. I have always told my family that the media can beat things up for ratings, whereby they exaggerate the truth or omit certain parts that don't fit the headlines.

Obviously, you can't believe everything you read in the papers or see on TV. An example of this is where the media may report a horrific murder, when a woman was walking home after dinner with friends, and was strangled. They elude that this was random act, and this has everybody running scared and talking about it around the water cooler.

Would you think of this headline a little differently, if they reported that she was with her husband, they had been drinking, and he choked her after having an argument? Or when they report that a child was kidnapped, forced into a car by a male outside the child's school and driven off into the distance.

Parents would be going into panic mode, and possibly keeping their kids home from school. Again, would you see this a little differently if the abductor was his father? Now I am not saying the murderer and the kidnapper are justified in their actions, I am merely trying to point out that the omission of certain details, that seem minor, can skew the public perception.

Yep, I chose this life and this wild, unpredictable ride. I put myself in harm's way, and I loved every bit of it. I took my old bank life, flipped the script, and did something completely opposite. The stuff I learned on the street was from the academy of life, and it's not something you can learn, other than by just doing it.

Whilst those experiences were not all pleasant, I had found my place. I now lived a life of crime, but I was on the good side. The people on the street, well, that's another story coming up next. You will be shocked, disgusted and amazed by what your fellow humans get up to.

CHAPTER THREE

Human 'Mis'behavior

Human beings can be dirty, disgusting, and do incredibly shocking things. Not everyone was raised with manners and social etiquette but shit, some people act like they have been brought up by aliens. It never ceased to amaze me, the actions people take to avoid capture or avoid police altogether.

People will do some stupid, random, crazy shit when they are under pressure, or forced to engage with police. When you are a cop, you will see that people lie, fight, throw stuff, hit you, and everything that you can imagine in between, to avoid interacting with police.

Lies, Lies, Lies

There are three sides to every story. His, hers, and the truth is somewhere in between. People tell lies. No really, they do, even to police. And some people are fantastic liars, that will attempt to steer your investigation off into the wrong direction. Luckily after doing this job for a while, it is easy to spot when someone is being untruthful.

You develop intuition when you see similar situations over and over, and watch the ways in which people behave. It's not just the bad guys that tell lies either, witnesses also lie, either to minimize their own involvement or to protect someone else. It is an offense to make a false statement in court and perjure yourself, but unfortunately, it's not a crime to lie to police. If it was, everybody would get thrown in the lockup at some stage.

Over the years, I have seen some criminals that surprisingly have morals, and others have none. Some suspects have absolutely no respect for authority or the uniform, and will challenge you every step of the way. Let's take the lying one step further, and make false allegations against police just for fun.

People crack the shits when they don't get their own way, or you tell them something they don't want to hear, so their defense is to make a false complaint. Usually of the nature that someone hit them, planted drugs on them, or tried to touch them inappropriately. If a civilian commits a crime, or makes a complaint, they are deemed innocent until proven guilty.

Unfortunately for a police officer, it is the other way around. Shit sticks and closely. If a police officer is accused of doing something wrong, they are guilty until proven innocent. It's a fact. It's not fair or just, but I guess it is because police are held to a higher standard than the average scumbag.

Just to be clear, I don't classify every person that commits a crime, as a scumbag. Good and decent people unfortunately commit crimes too, for a variety of reasons, but trust me, you know scum when you see it.

Signal One

Some people are just out to cause trouble, and stir shit just for fun. I can think of a time when a guy's troublemaking behavior turned deadly. I was working an evening shift in the city, when I heard three beeps in a row come over the police radio. This does not happen every day.

Usually if the radio operators had some urgent information to impart on the patrol officers, you would hear two beeps. When you hear three, this is called a Signal One, in my department at least, which means drop everything you are doing and get there now. It is normally used if an officer is shot or down, and we heard them sometimes when international flights were coming in to land, if there was a risk of the plane crashing.

Signal One is a big deal.

Police radio dispatchers called a Signal One, stating that an officer was down, and had been shot. Every car from the district began heading to the location. As we all raced to get there a drunken man had stepped off the curb and out into the traffic.

He was hit by the detectives' car and killed on the spot. The sad thing is, the Signal One turned out to be a hoax. Some idiot had stolen a portable radio, and pretended to be a downed officer. We never found out who did it.

At Their Worst

Police see people at their worst. Let's face it, rarely do police attend because anything good has happened. We turn up when shit happens, and people will say and do things that they normally wouldn't, especially when they are upset. But they are not attacking you personally, they are pissed off at the sight of the uniform.

This can also spill over to other emergency services personnel, and our paramedics at the time used to wear blue shirts. They changed to white, because people were mistaking them for police and attacking them.

Drugs, alcohol, and mental health issues also play a major role in how affected people conduct themselves. Depending on the severity of their condition, they can have superhuman strength and be capable of doing things that they normally couldn't or wouldn't.

Drug users will do anything to get what they need, and will rarely let anything come between them and their drugs. I have seen drug users that have injected alcohol when they have run out of gear, sometimes being fatal. Drug addicts will inject themselves in strange places to avoid having track marks on their arms, such as under the fingernails, between the toes, and even in the genitals.

I have been to many incidents where an offender is drug affected or having a psychotic episode. It can be disturbing to watch. I attended a call at a men's shelter where a female had been turned away, due to them having no beds. We approached her, and she was foaming at the mouth like a rabid dog, screaming at the top of her lungs and threatening everyone with a broken bottle.

We tried to draw her attention away from the staff and drew our batons. My partner was standing closer to her than I was, and as she lunged at us with the broken bottle, he cracked her across the forearm and bent her arm like a fucking banana. We immediately subdued her and called an ambulance.

We attended the hospital and when they placed her in an exam room, she picked up a metal framed bed over her head and was smashing the windows to get out. Superhuman strength at work, and she obviously felt no pain despite her screwed up arm. I have also seen people get shot, pepper sprayed, and hit with a baton, and just laughed.

Say What Now?

There are also certain phrases that most cops have heard from criminals, at one time or another throughout their career. Some of my all-time favorites and my usual responses include:

- "You've got the wrong person, it wasn't me." Sure, dickhead, you are on camera.
- "You're arresting me for no reason." Yep, you got me.

- "You have nothing better to do." Yep, I love to spend hours doing paperwork.
- "This is police harassment." Maybe you're right, I don't have anything better to do.
- "Take off your uniform and let's see how tough you are." But I just ironed my shirt.
- "Take off these cuffs and I will fucking kill you." Okay, how long will this take?
- "I will get you kicked off the force." Oh cool, I am sick of this job.
- "You fucking pigs are all corrupt." Well, the secret's out, what now?
- "I know my rights" OR "I know the law." Good, can you explain it to me?
- "I'll see you in court." Great, it's a date then.
- "I was gonna be a cop." Yeah, you don't say.
- "I pay my taxes, you work for me bitch." You pay taxes, so you have a job?

Not If.......When

With all this craziness flying around, most cops will tell you it's not a matter of *if* you get injured, it's *when*. We were told in no uncertain terms at the academy, that we will be injured at some point. We will get assaulted or attacked and it comes with the territory. That is completely true.

I am only speaking from my experience here, but I don't know any cops that have been on the force a while, that have never sustained any type of injury. When you are dealing with unpredictable and dangerous types on the daily, things are bound to happen unless you have a desk job. Not sure if paper cuts count, but a cop never getting injured, is like a doctor never getting blood on them. Just can't happen, especially for frontline officers.

I have had injuries, luckily mostly minor, but some of my colleagues were not so lucky. Most commonly, police get hit, punched, kicked, sworn at, and generally subjected to abuse. This is fairly standard behavior, and totally expected when dealing with the criminal element.

But occasionally you get hit with other things, or objects get thrown which can cause a little more tension than normal. I have been in riots and had house bricks and Molotov cocktails thrown at the patrol car, I have had boiling water thrown up my back when handing out prisoner meals in the police cells, and been hit with a bloodied tampon. Yes, it was still warm. So gross.

Sometimes it is not you that gets hit, and people take out their frustrations on your car. I remember a time when I was driving a police van through Chinatown in Sydney, and this drunk idiot walked up and punched the windscreen, smashing it right in front of my face. My partner jumped out in shock, and I parked the van and got out.

I grabbed the portable radio to call for backup, as he began fighting with my partner. Then I heard a blood curdling scream. I saw this guy's teeth sunk into my partner's arm, he wouldn't let go and he was drawing blood. I went over, and fearing that I would hurt myself as I was just getting over a sprained wrist from another job, I whacked him upside the head with the radio. He let go.

Fist fights are common place as a cop, and crooks just like to take their chances I suppose, but they usually come off second best. I couldn't count how many fights I have had, wrestling on the ground with suspects trying to cuff them, then there's the tackles, headlocks and everything in between.

I can handle myself as much as the next cop, and I am not one to back away from a fight, an arrest, an arm bar takedown or a leg sweep. Where I do draw the line is body fluids. Now there are times when said body fluids get on you by accident, and that is one thing, but when they get on you intentionally, I lose my shit.

I have had someone cut their wrists and wipe the blood on me, been spat on in the face, had semen thrown, yes, I know, gross and how the fuck did that happen? Some guy was wanking himself and didn't want to stop when we turned up. Of course, we were not keen to run up to him, but he finished himself and shared the outcome.

I feel sick even recounting that one. Sorry to say, but some people can do some filthy things. Some guys will stick their junk in just about anything you can think of, including animals or inanimate objects and some women will shove just about anything up where it ain't supposed to go. Their folks must be so proud.

When you work in the inner-city, you see all types, and anything goes. Just take a walk through the numerous sex shops, with dildos as big as your arm, and clear plastic toilet chairs, that you can stick your head under, to have your face pissed and shit on. I am not judging the things consenting adults do. Whatever blows your hair back.

These things are real, I am not even kidding, and I have not only seen them in those shops, I have seen them in people's homes, whilst they proudly tell you about using them. And what am I doing trolling through sex shops in uniform? Yes, people steal and damage shit from those places too.

More Body Fluids

Then of course, let's not forget there is vomit, piss, snot, and even shit. Personally, I gotta say shit is the worst. We had a nutjob that lived in the city area who was well known to every officer in the district, and even over in the neighboring areas. Why? Well, he was dubbed the Phantom Shitter.

This guy had HIV, and he was as mad as a cut snake. He was also the heir to an absolute fortune from a well-known beverage company. But he had a special talent. He could literally shit on command when stopped by police. He would shit his pants, then reach down and grab out a turd and throw it at the cops.

A whole new level of disgusting. I encountered this creep several times, but I knew his game, so I was lucky enough over the years to avoid the shit show. No pun intended. He did however, throw a handful of crap at some cops in a neighboring area, and it got into their mouths. They had to be tested for HIV.

It is not just the men that are gross, oh no. Women can be just as filthy and I have seen that first hand. I already mentioned getting freshly used tampons thrown at me, but have also had used condoms, bloodied bandages, and used syringes come at me. Again, it pains me to say that this is fairly "normal" in the cop world.

But there is one incident that stands out above the rest that cannot be unseen, and I will likely never get over it. Okay, I am being dramatic, but you be the judge. I arrested a known prostitute for drug possession and warrants. We took her back to the station, after dragging her out from under the police car.

She had dived under there and tried to hide her drugs in the car chassis. Anyway, after asking her nicely to come out, we escorted her to the police station and placed her in the dock. The dock area was basically a locked cage, with a solid metal frame and Perspex instead of bars for safety.

After watching her kick the Perspex constantly and scream about police brutality, we told her that we would need to get her out and fingerprint her. I distinctly remember her words back to us. "You will never get my prints, you cunts, you already fucking have them, every time I get arrested." The charging officer explained that we fingerprint and photograph every time, for every offense, to make sure these charges get attached to their criminal record.

After a few more attempts at telling us to fuck off, she pulled down her pants and shoved her hand up herself, pulled her hand out, and wiped it down the Perspex whilst stating, "Now try and fingerprint me, you cunts." Uggghhhhhh. Another cringe moment. We waited until after her morning shower for the prints.

But she got hit by the karma truck. Actually, she got hit by me. As we got her out of the cell to do the prints, I was standing behind her, and she turned her head and bit the escorting officer on the arm. She wouldn't let go, and sunk her teeth further into him, breaking the skin.

I punched her in the jaw, only once, and knocked her out. We put her back in the cell in the recovery position, then called for medical attention just in case. She came round and during an interview later with detectives, she kept complaining about her jaw being sore, but she couldn't remember why. What is it with these fuckwits wanting to bite all the time?

Can't Fix Stupid

Our fellow humans are feral creatures at times, and people are shocked and amazed when I tell some of my cop stories. I guess it is hard to believe that people can act like something from outer space. I don't want to say they act like animals, because I find animals are more civilized than humans at times. People will continue to do stupid things, when dealing with police and this will never change.

Maybe spare a thought for a cop next time you see one, and think about all the crap they have had to deal with from people, in some cases, quite literally. You could be excused for thinking that this is enough crazy behavior for anyone to put up with, and that's just from the living. Wait till you see what bizarre, and gruesome shit goes down with the dead.

CHAPTER FOUR

Death Becomes Everyone

Death unfortunately is a part of everyday life. It happens to the best of us, well actually it happens to all of us. Some people grow old gracefully, and slip away to a better place during their night time dreams. Others may not be so lucky, when they are called to their final destination. I can't list all the deaths, murders, and suicides I have been to. It would take too long.

Some people die horrific and gruesome deaths, some are tragic and downright sad, and others are so fucking ridiculous that you can't help but laugh. As promised earlier, this chapter is all about death. Everybody knows there are so many ways that people die every day, but death is such a major part of police work, that it gets its own chapter.

What is a Deaden?

When I first started on the force, before the AIDS guy, I remember other officers talking about "deadens" and how one officer was dubbed the "Angel of Death" because he had attended twenty in one month. I soon realized we were talking about a deceased, and I was shocked that he had attended so many deaths in such a short span of time.

What did a busload of tourists crash into a light pole? Did a football team get gunned down in the park? I fucking freaked out. I was twenty years old. I had never seen a dead guy before. Is this what I will have to deal with every day? I started to panic. Fear of the unknown, and hoping against hope that I would not be knee deep in dead bodies like he was.

Luckily, even for a busy inner-city station, that was considered out of the ordinary, and especially for the one officer. And now, just in case you were wondering, they were all single incidents. I don't know whether he was purposely volunteering, and trying to break some record, or whether he was just plain unlucky. I knew it would be part of my job. I hoped it wouldn't be as big a part as that.

Now don't get me wrong, the dead can't hurt us, but when you are young like I was at the time, it is confronting and it reminds you that we all eventually die. Interestingly, even as I went through the years as a cop, whenever I would respond to a call for a deceased, it filled me with dread, particularly in the case of children.

But sometimes the dying are scarier than the dead. When they are dead, it is all over, when they are dying and gasping for air, groaning, bleeding and taking their last breath, that is different altogether. Early in my career I had been called to a minor car crash. There was limited information about the scene, but we got there as soon as we could, expecting it to be just another accident.

Dying is Worse Than Dead

Some young guys had been driving too fast and ran into a large tree. As I got out of the patrol car, I couldn't believe what I was seeing. It was a cold night, and the steam from the radiator of the car was billowing out, and I could smell burnt rubber and brakes. The driver's side of the car was completely caved in, and the driver, was still suspended around the throat by his seatbelt, but was sitting in the dirt, covered in blood. I will never forget this scene.

He was making a growling noise, unconscious, and bleeding profusely. My partner took out his duty knife and cut the seatbelt. Then I saw his legs. He had no shoes on. One foot was completely split down the middle from his toes to his ankle. The other leg was totally fucked, and wrapped completely around the back of him.

His friend was not so lucky. His side of the car had no damage at all, yet he was dead in the passenger seat. He had no visible injuries, other than a small amount of blood coming out the back of his head, and he was clutching the seatbelt. Against all odds, the driver survived to live a life in a wheelchair. They were both seventeen.

Delivering Death

One of the hardest things a cop can ever do, is deliver a death message to a person's loved ones. It doesn't get any easier, even when you've done it plenty. Imagine a stranger coming to your door, telling you the worst possible news about your loved one. Obviously, it is very common for family members not to believe what you are telling them, and they react in all different ways.

Police are not being cruel when they blurt out that "Johnny is dead." We are trained to get straight to the point, because people in that state get confused. If you say the victim has been fatally injured, all they hear is injured, and then ask if they will be okay. It seems cruel, but you must be blunt so there is no confusion.

Death Message With a Side of Murder

I once went to a woman's home who was babysitting her infant grandson. It was one o'clock in the morning, and I woke her and told her that her daughter was dead. She had been murdered. She let out the most chilling and painful scream, one that I will never forget.

We had been searching for her daughter after she failed to return home from work. My partner and I found her in a shopping center carpark, dead in her mother's car. She had her throat cut, and her head almost completely severed. Her husband had killed her. This was a case of domestic violence gone to the extreme.

Suicide

Murder is unfortunately a very distinct part of the job. It is the ultimate sin. It is more than just a death, it is a death at the hand of someone else, and I have seen more than I can recall. But what if the death is at the hands of the victim themselves? Yes, suicide. Another huge part of the job of policing.

It never ceases to amaze me, the ways in which people take their own life. Obviously, drug overdoses, cutting wrists, hanging, shooting yourself, and jumping from buildings are fairly common. Other less common ways that I have personally seen, are people jumping in front of trucks, a fifteen-year-old boy who laid his neck down on the train tracks because people thought he was gay, and a guy who drank a bottle of acid.

Then there's the phenomenon of suicide by cop, whereby a person wants to die so they will do some bad shit, like create a hostage or siege situation and confront police, hoping to be taken out. There are many ways to take your own life, and I have seen many more than outlined here. Too many to list.

Death Without Dignity

With all this death talk, have you ever wondered what actually happens when you die? Well as if dying isn't bad enough, your body can do some really weird things after you go. Like what, you ask? Well, it turns out mom needn't have been so insistent on you wearing clean underwear, in case you get into an accident.

Chances are, if you die, you are going to shit yourself anyway. And piss. It's a sobering thought, but the muscles that control the sphincter of the bowel and bladder completely relax upon death, as there is nobody to control them. Doesn't always happen, like if they had recently been to the bathroom, but mostly. But that's not the only thing that can happen.

When the brain is switching off, the muscles can twitch and spasm making it appear that the person is still alive. And just in case you've heard rumors, a guy can get one last erection, not even kidding. I have seen this myself (the muscle twitching, not the last erection, let's be clear), and almost made the rookie mistake of saying to the paramedics, "oh look he's alive."

Many a morgue attendant could tell a tale about a dead person moving. Then there's the moaning and groaning sounds, which is generally air or gases being expelled from the body. Again, very disconcerting and takes a bit of getting used to.

One Man, Two Hookers, and a Dildo

Upon death, a person's eyes can be fully opened, or they can naturally rest partially opened, due to the muscles relaxing. But eyes can also seemingly open up, which again is due to muscle twitches as the body is shutting down. Now, I could tell you one of my stories here about this very thing happening, but in all fairness, my husband, Jason, who was also a cop, had a story that I just cannot beat, so here goes:

He was a young rookie working in a red-light district in Sydney. He and his partner got called to a very expensive apartment building in a fancy suburb of the inner city, for a deceased. When he got there, he saw a dead guy in the bed, with two transgender prostitutes in the room. He noticed the guy was married, as he had a wedding ring on his finger.

He asked the two people what happened, and at first, they were acting weird and said they didn't know. Upon pressing them a little further, they revealed that they had picked him up in a bar and brought him to their home for sex. Apparently one of them had shoved a dildo up his butt, and he had a heart attack and died.

As if this case wasn't strange and funny enough, as Jason and his partner continued to chat to these two witnesses, Jason looked over and saw the dead guy open his eyes. The two transgender hookers started screaming with joy that he was alive, until the paramedics explained that this was a normal post-death reaction.

Jason then went on to deliver the news to the guy's wife. As if it wasn't bad enough that they had to tell her he died, she kept begging to know what happened. They warned her that she would be shocked, and it was not pleasant, but she demanded to know. So, his partner told her. He said they could still hear her screaming when they got in the car to leave. *Shit!!!*

So How Do I Look?

It always amazed me when I would attend a scene for a deceased female, and the male officers would comment on her looks. They would discuss how it was such a shame that she was dead, because she was so pretty. What a stupid comment. The girl is dead. What, would it be okay if she was ugly?

So, after all the pleasantries of dying, there is more. After death you start to look all bruised up as the blood stops pumping around the body. It begins to pool in low lying areas, as there is no heart to pump it back through the body. This is referred to as lividity.

It can be scary to see the first time, for example, a person laying on their back will look normalish, but roll them over, and the back will look like it's covered in blood or bruises. It's just where the blood has pooled. Skip forward an hour or so and rigor mortis, or a stiffening of the body will start to set in.

This usually leaves the body after some time, and then we start to decompose. Well decomposition really starts to happen as soon as you die, but the body's tissues can die at different rates. Then, if you are not found in a reasonable amount of time, you will start to bloat.

The human body can blow up like a puffer fish, and can almost double in size due to the build-up of post mortem gases in the body. At this stage the skin usually starts to go black as well. Pretty gross. Stay with me.

Bloat and Blowflies

Then the active decay sets in, whereby every-thing starts to break down and become liquefied. This is particularly disgusting, especially when you get dead person juice on you. Oh yeah, this happens, but thankfully it never happened to me. Remember, body fluids and I don't mix.

I was working in a country station with a crusty old sergeant, and we got called to a house where the man hadn't been seen for a week. It was the middle of summer, so I was thinking the worst. Once we arrived at the house, this was confirmed as the front window of the home was covered in blowflies. *Fuck !!*

Once we got out of the patrol car, the stink hit me. The smell of death is an unmistakable smell. Imagine that disgusting, rotting meat smell when you drive past roadkill. Now times that by ten, purely because you know it's human. I would rather be anywhere else.

The house was locked up tight, and the sergeant found an axe by the back door. He chopped down the door and we went in. I took a huge breath and went through there as fast as I could. We got to the front of the house with the fly covered windows, and there he was; all black, puffed up, and leaking fluid where the skin had split.

Not much we could do for him, so we went outside to call for crime scene photographers. The smell was so fucked. I could taste it. I felt like it was in my mouth, and I must have spit in the front yard about twenty-five times. Sights I can handle, smells I cannot.

Autopsy

The final piece of the death puzzle is the autopsy. Another lovely part of the job, but I promise the next chapter will be a little lighter. I remember attending my first autopsy in the city morgue. I was so nervous, my heart was pounding, and of course, the place stunk of heavy, death chemicals that got in your clothes.

An autopsy is completed for every death, unless the person has been suffering from a life-threatening condition within the past few months, and a doctor is willing to write a death certificate. Remember my AIDS death? That was a doctor's certificate. Turns out it should have been an autopsy, with the murder allegations flying around.

So, they cut the scalp and peel it right back, then get an electric saw, cut the top of the skull, and pop it off to expose the brain. They also cut down through the sternum and using rib spreaders, pull the ribcage apart to access those organs.

Organs are generally removed, weighed, measured and samples taken before being placed back in the body, then everything is sewn back up like a chaff bag. All of this to determine the cause of death, and sometimes, you don't get one.

Death is the great equalizer and it befalls us all one way or another. There are no good deaths as such, but the best death story I ever heard was of an old guy in his early nineties, still riding ranch work. He took ill, stepped down from his horse, got down on the ground, crossed his ankles, crossed his hands over his chest and died. Now, that's the kind of death I would like to have.

But we don't get that choice, unless we take our own life. Some people die in awful circumstances, and others die in just plain weird settings. You can't change it, you can't stop it, so you might as well live large while you still can, which leads me to how cops cope with the demands of the job.

CHAPTER FIVE

What It Takes To Wear The Badge

Police work is gritty, dirty, and hard. It takes a certain kind of person to put up with the types of work that we have already looked at. These events are not just a one off, they are day in day out, in the life of a cop. It can become a grind.

Just because you got a death job today, doesn't mean you won't get another one tomorrow. And the day after, or even the same day. But there are ways that police handle situations, to be able to cope with this stuff on the daily, and it helps to have some of the following traits.

Keep Your Shit Together

So now you have had a little taste of the kind of incidents I attended every day, I wanted to touch on how cops do what they do. Day after day. Year after year. Policing is not just a job, it is a career, and it's one that can have a very short shelf life if you don't take care of yourself.

You are not going to be much good to anybody, if you go to pieces every time shit gets real. And you better forget your visions of grandeur and wanting to change the world. You can't and you won't. That doesn't mean for one minute that you shouldn't try, but unless every criminal only committed one crime and learnt their lesson, police will never be out of a job.

You won't change the world, and you can only focus on the task in front of you and do your best each time. In doing so you will feel fulfilled and rewarded for your efforts in keeping the streets safe. But with all that you put into policing, you have to be careful that it doesn't take everything from you.

Being a cop is a needy kind of occupation. It takes and takes and takes from you, sometimes to the point where officers have no more to give. So to be a really good cop, you need to protect yourself first, both physically and mentally.

You are not going to be much good to anyone if you are not coping with the work. To be the best, you have to protect yourself. First and foremost, I strongly believe that physical fitness is key. When I joined the force, I remember thinking that I owe it to myself to be as fit as possible.

How can I put my body on the line, chase the bad guys, wrestle crooks and keep the public safe, if I am not fit myself? Being fit is more important though than just having the upper hand, and getting the gold medal for kicking ass. Being fit is not just for handcuffing someone in record time, and catching them in a foot pursuit.

It can be a matter of life and death. No bullshit. Okay, this might sound dramatic so let me explain. If I walk into a bar fight, and get jumped by a person who is trying their best to overpower me, I would want to have a certain level of fitness to deal with that. Or if I was wrestling a suspect who was resisting arrest and could push me into the traffic, I would at least want to be strong and fit.

And of course, there is the risk of being overpowered and having the suspect try to take your gun. You could see how badly that could turn out. It is no guarantee that fitness and strength will save you, but I would rather be capable than not.

Staph Infections and Strip Searches

But protecting yourself is not just about being a picture of fitness. There are other hazards that cops need to be aware of, that could impact their own health. Two chapters back I spoke about people throwing shit, vomit, blood, and every other body fluid at cops. Well further to all that mess, is the risk of contracting lice, scabies, staph infections, diseases and being exposed to open wounds with fuck-knows-what germs in them.

And yes, I have a nasty story about doing a strip-search on a very large female. This lovely lady was arrested and brought into the station for charging. I was working in the charge room that day, so it was my job to strip-search her, as she had warrants and would be staying for a few nights with us in the cells.

She stank, she had crusty dry shit in her pants, she hadn't showered since who knows when, her socks could have walked the hall by themselves and the general odor was ominous. Cast your mind back to when I said I hated bad smells, like with the blowfly guy, and you can imagine my disgust being in a locked private room with her.

I was almost dry heaving, and decided to get this over as quick as possible. She had warrants for failing to appear in court on drug possession charges, so I knew I had to at least have a bit of a decent look as to where she may hide something. I was somewhat scared, and the smell was sickening.

After getting her to take her clothes off, and doing the proverbial squat and check to see if she had anything shoved between her cheeks, I had to ask her to lift her tits so I could check under them. Like I said, she was a very, very large lady so she had a lot of big, old, droopy boob going on.

She lifted them and out drops a bag of pot, cash, a credit card and sanitary pads that she had placed under there to soak up the sweat. When the pads dropped away, holy shit. She was covered in big, weeping, yellow sores and promptly said she has had a "bit of staph."

What in the actual fuck did I just see? I wanted to scratch my own eyes out. I asked why she had the cash and all that crap stored under her tits and she told me, "I don't like carrying a bag." You just can't make this shit up.

Remain Detached

Apart from the physical, cops also need to protect themselves emotionally and mentally. So how do you do that when you are seeing tragedy all the time? Well it helps to remain detached. You need to build up a hard shell and adopt a "better them than me" attitude. Some people will call you cold and heartless, but remaining detached is the only way to really preserve your own self.

You can do your job and be empathetic and understanding, but you cannot emotionally involve yourself in other people's problems. Getting overly invested in people's misery and tragedy is a sure-fire fast track to your own downfall. Have you ever wondered why you see cops on the news laughing at a horrific murder scene? They are protecting themselves.

Humor is a coping mechanism for cops. Sure, it is probably not a good look on TV to see a bunch of cops laughing whilst standing by a dead guy, but it can be a coping mechanism. The longer you have been a cop, the more hardened you become. Some cops could just be genuinely not bothered by the scene, but those with less experience are encouraged to use humor as a weapon to defend themselves.

Another way to remain detached is to justify it as being the victim's own fault in some way. For example, if you are seeing someone stabbed and bleeding to death, it is easier if he was a scumbag anyway, than if it was a random innocent person. Before you raise up in your seat, I am not saying anyone deserves to die.

Criminals are people too and they have family, and I am merely saying that it is a way for police to cope with seeing this stuff daily. Police see so many gruesome scenes that can't be unseen, so it is paramount to keep yourself separate from the situation, and find any way you can to do this.

Stay Sharp

Police also have great insight into human behavior, and quickly learn how to read people and situations. This is due to seeing the same types of behaviors over and over, and while individuals can certainly be unpredictable, there are some aspects that you will come to expect and see regular behavioral patterns.

Because people are so unpredictable, situations can go from bad to worse in a heartbeat so you learn to think on your feet, make split-second decisions and adjust accordingly. And, split-second decisions can mean the difference between life and death. Police need to have their wits about them at all times.

You need to know your surroundings and who is in them. This is not the type of job where you want to turn up hungover or rolling in from a big night out. Things can go to shit in the blink of an eye and you have to be prepared for that. Cops don't trust anyone they deal with, not if they are smart.

Like I said, when you deal with people all day every day, you get to learn all about human behavior, and therefore you develop a strong intuition which helps in investigating crime. I always trust my gut instincts, and my bullshit meter, which were both very well developed over time.

Gut Instincts

Think back to the guy that murdered his wife in the carpark. We had been looking for her, after she failed to come home after work. She had been living with her mom since she had split from her husband. As a matter of routine, we had to go to the home that she shared with him previously, and ask him if he had seen her that day.

It was about eight o'clock at night, but it was daylight savings time so it was still light outside. At this time, she had only been missing a short while, so we had no major alarm bells ringing just yet. I walked up to the house and knocked on the door, he answered and invited us into the home.

I asked him if he had seen his estranged wife and he obviously said he hadn't. He was cool and calm, and answered all my questions, no problem. But I felt something was not quite right. I thanked him for his time, and as we got into the patrol car I got my police notebook out and started to write notes.

I wrote notes on his demeanor, observations on what he was wearing, how the house looked and how it appeared he had attempted to hide his car. I don't know what made me write all those notes, but I just had a feeling that something was not right. We would come to find out later, that when we were standing casually in his living room, he had already murdered her a few hours before.

Even after I left the force, after fifteen years, I realized you can take the girl out of the force, but you can't take the force out of the girl. The skills you learn as a cop never leave you and sometimes people will still ask me if I am a cop, just because of the way I stand or carry myself.

Police are naturally curious and suspicious creatures because they have to be. They need to be curious enough to ask questions, and suspicious enough to not be blindly trusting. When I was a cop it was important to know my surroundings, and this has carried through for me today. Most cops cannot take someone standing behind them. I still can't stand it to this day.

I fucking *hate* when I go to the cinema, and I strategically position myself to where I can see most people. I sit where I can see the room and the exits, as far away from others as I can, and then someone sits right behind me. I hate it. It makes me nervous and more often than not, I will get up and move.

I think it is so ingrained to keep your wits about you, that it is just a hard habit to break. I don't care, I am happy with it. I know who is around me, and I prefer to see what people are doing in front of me, not wondering what they are doing behind me. Hopefully I will see something before someone else does and get out of there if needed.

People always ask me if I was ever scared as a cop. I would have to say a resounding "No." Call me arrogant, call me stupid, but I trusted myself, my training, my skills and abilities. I was lucky enough to always feel like I could handle myself, read a situation, and not get too beat up.

Sure, I would feel the adrenaline kick in, and would be hyper-vigilant to situations, but not fearful. Funny enough, a crazy, angry person in front of me doesn't scare me, even with weapons. I was more fearful of the unknown, like when I first saw dead bodies.

I recall one girl that died, who was sitting upright on the floor, leaning against a mattress, with her eyes open. She had a pet rat in a cage, disgusting, and all I could think of was that filthy rodent getting out and chewing on her. I hate creepy shit, but angry people—no problem.

Always a Cop

If you know any police officers and have ever seen them off duty at a party, barbecue, or in a bar you will know what I mean by this next bit. The cop will be there scoping the place out, seeing where the exits are, who is in the room and where. And then they will be likely to stand in a direction where they can see the crowd in case shit goes down.

I am guilty of that myself. I also still drive my car with one hand on the seat belt clip. I don't consciously choose to do it, it just happens. This comes from years of being a patrol officer, whereby you sometimes have to exit your vehicle in a hurry. You can't exit the car without removing the seat belt. Still a habit of mine to this day.

And then there are certain songs that will trigger memories from major crimes that I have attended. It may be as simple as the next song you hear on the radio after attending a difficult crime scene. I can literally not think about that job for years, but if I hear that song, it reminds me of it. Strange how the mind works sometimes, and attaches certain triggers that take you right back to the crime scene.

Police work is grimy, stressful and sometimes it's hard to leave the things behind that you see at work. But you need to make that distinction to protect yourself. It takes guts, balls, bravery, and boldness to be a cop, and this job is not for the timid or for those with weak stomachs. It just isn't. It takes a certain kind of person to do this job, especially for any length of time.

You have to be resilient and just reboot each day and start anew. Leave work at work. This applies regardless of whether officers are men or women, but there are some things that come up on the job that are specific to females, and I bet you are dying to know what they are, so read on.

CHAPTER SIX

The "Other" F Word: Female

Men and women can be equally as good as each other at policing. This we already know, but women have some other situations that arise that are specific to being female. Policing is still a male-dominated occupation, and many women probably mistakenly think they could not do the job. Nothing could be further from the truth.

Women make good cops, and they have certain traits and skills that can work in everyone's favor. And you don't have to be single, childless, big, and act like a man to make it as a cop. I am not a feminist, by any means, as I grew up with a brother, and lived in a small lakeside town, where most kids my age were boys.

I climbed trees, went fishing, rode a horse and a skateboard and built cubby houses in the woods. I was a tomboy, so it wasn't a big leap to then take a male-dominated career path, and carve out my place there. While I am not a feminist, I firmly believe that women are as good as male officers.

Though I do believe in gender equality in the force, there are certain aspects of policing that are specific to females. I have never had any major issues—as I have always stood up for myself—but being female does bring unique situations. When I was in elementary school in the 1970s, I remember female police officers or as we called them "lady policemen" giving us talks on stranger danger.

Funnily enough, later I got called the same thing when I was on the force. Either that or people would point out that you were a "girl cop." But back in the 1970s, women mainly worked in the traffic section as part of the school lecturing branch. They carried a leather satchel-type bag with their traffic ticket book inside.

It wasn't too many years before then, that women had to leave the force if they got married. It was only in 1961 that the New South Wales Police Force allowed women to stay in the department after marriage.

That's why all the top ranking female officers were never married and had no children. Back then they had to choose marriage and kids or a career as a cop. Not both. Can you imagine being told to leave the force nowadays because you got married?

Female Advantages

While I would never play on being a female cop, there are some distinct advantages to having female officers on the force. When you consider that approximately 50% of the population is female, it stands to reason that female officers should be equally represented. But the stark reality is, they are not.

Now I am not going to quote statistics here because by the time I write them, they will likely change, but mostly women are drastically outnumbered by men. An advantage of having female officers is that they are usually good at communicating with female victims of crimes, such as domestic violence and sexual assault.

Don't get me wrong here, and I don't want any hate mail, as men can equally do the same job, but in my experience, I have found that women and children of such crimes can be more comfortable talking to a female officer, if one is available.

I want to strongly state that this is not always the case, but something I have certainly found. Female officers are also utilized for strip-searching female suspects, to search for drugs or other illegal items, like with my tits-as-a-bag lady.

Sometimes, female officers do not possess the general strength of male officers, therefore they are usually good communicators, and relying on this tool is paramount. I have also found that male suspects can react better to a female officer in some situations, and most maintain some level of respect (maybe like they are talking to their mother).

This is not always the case, but certainly something I have experienced. Some male suspects just don't do well with a big tough guy telling them what to do. Sometimes it starts out well and ends up in a pissing match, so female officers can be effective in calming things down.

Women can also be utilized for undercover operations, where a female is likely going to be beneficial to the case. For example, very early in my career, I was approached by our regional drug squad to go undercover, in an escort service. I jumped at the chance.

Then, when I thought about it a bit more, I couldn't help but wonder exactly what they would want me to do. Not to worry, as the commander refused to let me do it, stating that it was far too risky. Good call.

Female Disadvantages

With advantages come *dis*advantages. As I said before, some women are not as strong as men. Now I am a tall, fit, and strong 5'10" woman, but men can still have the edge in the strength department. Have I overpowered men? Absolutely. Have men overpowered me? Absolutely, and that's where I have to resort to other tactics to get the upper hand.

That's where you have to be smart and use your communication skills. Of course, tasers, batons, guns, and pepper spray help too, but sometimes you are not respected as a female, and some suspects might not want to deal with a woman. No big deal, they don't have a choice anyway.

I did find in the earlier days of my career, I had to work twice as hard for half the respect that the guys got. As time went on, I either got the respect or didn't give a fuck anyway. Most women even today would likely go into the force still feeling that sense of having to prove themselves, because it is still a male domain.

There are also misconceptions about female police, whereby some may think women are too soft to do the job, that they will cry when something bad happens, or worry about breaking a nail or changing their tampon. Yeah, just fuck off.

There is also the stereotype that all female officers are either bitches or sluts. Heard this many, many times. Suspects just assume when they see a female officer, that we are going to be bitchy and hard to deal with. Are there bitches out there on a power trip? Absolutely, but I was not one of them. I used to pride myself on being firm but fair.

And the slut thing…. women that join the force just want to be around a bunch of guys all the time, so they must be sluts. Yeah, *no*. I did *not* join the force for the men, please. When we were at the police academy all the girls were spoken to by our class mentor, a guy, who said that we will get hit on and harassed by guys.

I thought he was talking about suspects, but he was talking about the fucking cops. And yes, that happens, because women are still kind of a novelty in policing, but you teach people what your boundaries are, and make it clear from the start, that you are not a piece of ass to be chased around the station.

One last disadvantage to being a "lady policeman" is that sometimes it is inappropriate for a female officer to interact with men of certain cultures. Inappropriate on their part, not mine. I have had occasions where I was called to homes for different reasons and not been allowed to enter the home, or speak to the male occupant. Again, sometimes they don't get a choice.

How I Met My Husband

So, I think I mentioned that my husband used to be a cop too. I joined the force three months before him, and left a few months after he did. He was in the class after me, so we were both at the academy for three of the six months at the same time, but we didn't know each other. I had been working in my first station for a few years, but it wasn't until I was posted to another city station that I met Jason.

I had been stationed there for a while, and I came into work one day and went into the sergeant's office to read the board, and see what my duties were that day. I see the patrol car written up, City 15, and my name, which was Nicholls back then, then I see Doble. I distinctly remember, like yesterday, saying to the old sarge, "Who the fuck is Doble?"

He told me that he was a new guy transferring in from another station. *Fuck me, this sucks, I hate working with people I don't know.* You just get so used to working with other officers, and then some new guy comes along and you have to get to know him. But he walked in the door, I think my mouth came open and I was like "wow." He was gorgeous, tall, dark, and handsome. So, my day just got better.

We worked on a team-based roster system, so we didn't have one designated partner, but instead would rotate through partnering up each day with someone from our team. Although I wished I could be his designated partner all the time. We worked together, sometimes on the same patrol car, sometimes on different cars, but always on the same shift, as we were on the same team.

Anyway, to cut a long sordid story very short, about three months later, we started seeing each other, and moved in together two weeks after that, and that was over twenty-five years ago. It definitely helps to be married to another cop. You understand what the other goes through, and you don't have to explain things too much.

I did keep my maiden name at work though, even after we were married, because I worked with Jason so often, I didn't want people asking if we were married or brother and sister. All through my career, Jason and I worked together at the same station, usually on the same team, and regularly on the same patrol car.

Yeah, imagine that, being married and working on the same car as your husband. Let that sink in for a bit. It was actually great, because we know how the other thinks, and I knew that he had my back 110%. The only downside was that we had to work twice as hard to prove that we weren't off somewhere making out in the car.

Married with Children

We eventually had three sons; Jack, Tom, and Joe, and at the time they were aged three and under. Shift work with kids can be tricky and does take a bit of planning, but you can do it. I did it for years. Jason and I worked twelve-hour shifts, either 6am to 6pm, or 6pm to 6am.

After we had kids, one would go to work at night, then come home, and high five as the other was on the way out the door for the day shift. Of course, there was a few minutes of handover time but our commander was always very supportive and flexible for us. This worked out fine, as I knew that if my kids were not with me, they were with their dad.

It was hard for the poor person that was on nights though, as you would get home and climb into bed, just as three little boys were waking up.

But we worked it out. And occasionally we would get our moms to come and watch them as we slept. Of course, shift work is not unique to policing, but it is a large part of it. There are plenty of moms and dads out there that are nurses, factory workers, or bar attendants that work nights too.

Men Behaving Badly

Any girl knows, that men sometimes will make rude comments, catcalls, and wolf whistles to get your attention. That doesn't stop when you are a cop, but you just ignore it. It happens to the guys too as some women go stupid when they see a guy in uniform.

But apart from that unwanted attention, and being called every conceivable derogatory name you can imagine, there was one standout, that I seemed to get called on a regular basis. I would get called a "black-haired slut." *Hmmm, so original.* I do have dark hair, but I am not sure how my hair has anything to do with it. Leave my hair out of this.

But that's not the worst thing I have been called. Apart from the usual suspects of "cunt, mole, bitch, slut, scum, and dog", there was the female-oriented comments, which were worse in reality, than what I have written here.

- "Don't break a fucking fingernail you bitch."
- "Do you have to go and change your tampon?"
- "I'm gonna fuck you until you bleed."
- "I'm gonna slit your throat and fuck the hole."
- "I'm gonna get all my buddies to come and gang-fuck you."
- "Wanna see my dick?" OR "Suck my dick."
- "All you female cops are fucking whores."

Obviously, this came from dickhead wankers that weren't happy with the service for some reason. *Too bad so sad.* Everyone—male or female—puts up with abuse, but the female officers in the city were subjected to abuse from within the ranks too—until I had something to say about it.

Police Doctor and Pervert

When all new officers joined, male or female, at some point you got sent to see the police medical officer. He would check your weight, height, heart rate, and general health usually after you graduated from the academy, and before going back for secondary training. The police medical officer was a crusty old pervert, that looked like he had been there a thousand years.

Imagine my surprise after hearing stories from other girls that had attended his office, who told me that you have to strip down to your underwear for the medical exam, and take off your bra. *Say what now?*I asked them to repeat as I could not believe what I was hearing. I asked them, "Why would you need to remove your bra?"And they said he told them it was to check their heartbeat. Please.

But, did they not think there was something wrong with that picture, really??? So......my turn. I go in and he does some of the mundane measurements, uh huh, then...... "Take your uniform off, everything off just down to your underpants, bra off too." I told him no and asked him what he would possibly need me to take my bra off for. He told me it was to check my heartbeat.

I told him—in no uncertain terms—that he could do that without me having my tits out, and he told me that he would report that I had not been compliant. I said, "Go your fucking hardest, I am reporting you for sexual misconduct." I did report him, and I told every girl I knew, about what had happened and what I did. From that day on, everybody refused to strip down and he eventually "retired."

Women make great police officers. When you think about women being approximately half of the world's population, it makes sense that women would be cops too. There are many suspects that are female, and it helps to have a female officer if they need a thorough search. A large portion of victims of domestic violence are women and kids, so again, female police can be very comforting to those people.

Dealing with the public can be quite challenging, regardless of the officer's gender. People can be misinformed and believe things about police that are not true. Next, I will explain myths and misconceptions—and wait till you read the common questions coming right up.

CHAPTER SEVEN

Myths, Misconceptions, and Common Questions

Myths

Policing is not a normal profession, and can be shrouded in mystery, so it stands to reason that people can be curious about what is real and what is rumor. The Hollywood movie industry has built up a picture of law enforcement that works for entertainment, but it is not a realistic view.

Hollywood has a certain formula to bring action and excitement to the big screen. Police also have a formula for action and excitement, it's just that it's completely different. Police work is real. There are many myths and urban legends about policing, and just as many misconceptions about what the job entails.

There are also common questions about procedure, and it is interesting to note the public's perception on policing. Hollywood has alot to answer for when it shows over the top car chases, crazy police launching their vehicles through the air, and my favorite, shooting a suspect and then walking off into the sunset.

It does not happen that way. A police-involved shooting is nothing like what is portrayed on TV. Apart from the death of the suspect being gruesome and bloody, remember they will likely piss and shit themselves, you can't just walk away and get a donut (I will come back to the donut situation).

The scene is usually volatile, the suspect is all messed up, police might be injured themselves or be at risk, and there is always screaming and high emotions. I can remember a particularly sad, police-involved shooting that I attended. I had been working in a country station, at a border town.

My shift that night was a ten-hour stretch, as we were conducting liquor licensing operations, and were due to finish at 4am. I was extremely happy to see 4am, after walking through all the local bars and restaurants, checking for liquor violations. I went into the locker room, just opened my locker door to start packing up for the night, when we got a frantic call from the station officer in the town just over the border.

Although it was a different state, we had jurisdiction in that town, and they in ours, being that we were on the border. This gave us the authority to legally enter the state and enact police powers. The young officer on the other end of the line was in extreme distress, and advised that his officers had just attended a domestic violence job, and they had shot someone.

We got the address from him and drove straight there. The scene was nasty. There was a woman lying dead in the driveway of the home, with a small bullet entry wound in her chest. Her back had been blown out by the hollow-point projectile ripping through her. There was a junior officer standing over the body, in complete shock. He could not move.

There was a senior officer who had locked herself in the police vehicle, due to a crowd of about twenty family and friends of the victim, threatening to kill her. There was also the woman's husband and two-year-old child kneeling by her side, crying and stroking her hair—and yes, she had pissed and shit herself.

They had gone to the home to respond to a domestic violence call, and the aggressor was not the man, but the woman. Apparently, she regularly attacked police after she had been drinking, as the officer had been there many times before. As they knocked on the door, she ran at them with two knives overhead, one in each hand, and chased them down the driveway.

They backed up as far as they could, and told her to stop or they would shoot, before both firing on her. So, you can see this shit is real, and Hollywood makes it look easy, and cool and seemingly no big deal. I can tell you it changed the lives of both those officers forever.

Another Hollywood myth is that all divisions in the police force, are constantly fighting with each other. Think of any cop movie you have seen. Usually, it is very clichéd, there is a drunk guy, they are divorced, and the patrol guys hate the detectives, who hate the traffic cops. I am not speaking for everyone here, but I have never seen that type of behavior.

Maybe some places are like that, but it's just not something that I have seen. Again, staying on the topic of Hollywood, I don't know any cop, anywhere, ever who would find drugs, cut them open, and taste them to see what they are. That is just complete and utter bullshit.

You would not "taste" an unknown substance that you just found on a scumbag, to see if it's cocaine, meth or heroin. There are some preliminary tests that can be done to determine if the substance is a narcotic, but essentially the drugs would go to a lab and be tested properly. Again, this is only in my experience, but I don't know any officer in their right mind that would risk ingesting an unknown substance.

Enough of bashing the movie industry, which I love by the way. I do like a well-produced crime thriller, but when stuff is way over the top I tune out. There is also a common myth that police have quotas to which they must meet regardless, and therefore do anything to anyone to meet them. In my police department, we did not have quotas.

We did have key performance indicators, but they were more for managing our case files and getting our court briefs filed. Highway patrol did not get tasked to go out and get a certain amount of tickets, but the theory is, that if a highway patrol officer is driving around for twelve hours a day, and doesn't come back with one ticket, then something is wrong.

You can't drive for that long, and not see one driver do the wrong thing. Not possible. In addition to the myth around quotas, people think that if they have a criminal record as a juvenile, it automatically gets wiped clean when they turn eighteen. There may be some states where this is true, but certainly not in mine or most.

The juvy record is still there, sometimes they can be locked away, but they are still there. Sometimes they still appear but can't be taken into account for adult charges, but again, still there. Some states may wipe a record clean, but beware, because it is a very common myth that a juvenile record is wiped clean, and that is generally not the case.

Another myth floating around is that police love talking about their work. No, they don't. To us it's a job. Would a hairdresser go out to dinner and talk about every haircut they had done that day, no they wouldn't, well maybe. To us, it's a tough job that drains your soul at times, and is just not something cops want to sit and chat over with people.

Now, talking about stressful or funny events to other cops is a different matter, but other cops have probably been there too and can understand what you go through. My pet fucking *hate,* I have a few, is going to social functions and people blurting out "Lisa is a cop" or now "Lisa was a cop." Really pisses me off, because if I wanted them to know I would tell them myself.

I do not think I am special or particularly interesting, and I don't like my job being the topic of focus at parties. Apart from not wanting my career to dominate the conversation, and be all about me, that's where it ends up going to. Then you get asked a million questions, and the spotlight goes on you. I am fairly low-key and not a fan of that, at all.

Misconceptions

Misconceptions are another large part of police work, and I aim to clarify some of those right now. One thing that any police officer would likely have been asked, many times, is "why don't you just shoot bad guys in the leg." The short answer is, it is extremely hard to shoot a moving target.

A leg is a smallish target to aim for in the heat of battle, when adrenaline is high, unless the suspect is standing still. Police are trained to stop the threat, and aim for the largest target, which is center body mass. If shit goes down, and you pull your gun, you can bet your ass that you are not going to follow a fucking leg in your gun sight.

Police are authorized to use deadly force when an imminent deadly threat is present, or they have a reasonable fear of being overpowered, which could lead to death. If a person is holding an axe and threatening to chop someone's head off, do you really want to pop him in the leg and still have the arms free, or do you want to lay him out on the ground?

It may seem like police are trained to shoot to kill, but it is more shoot to stop the threat, and if death occurs as a result, then so be it. The theory is if you are justified in pulling out your gun, and shooting it, then you are justified in killing the person. Your gun is absolutely your last resort.

False confessions are another major misconception, whereby people don't believe anybody would confess to a crime if they didn't do it. People do falsely confess and it is not uncommon. Sometimes innocent suspects confess for notoriety, to make a name for themselves, some do it due to mental confusion, believing they must have committed the crime, and some do it to take the heat off another person.

Others confess due to police interrogation tactics, and believe that the interrogation will stop if they just say they did it. Either way, physical and other evidence usually flushes them out, when details provided in the confession do not match evidence from the crime scene.

But there are many cases where the confession is wrongly held as the strength of the case, and therefore innocent people can get convicted. Closely tied into this misconception, is the belief that eyewitness testimony is accurate. Eyewitness evidence is notoriously inaccurate. Why?

Because people perceive situations very differently, by focusing on different aspects, which are then processed differently in the brain. If you had a group of people witness the same event, you would get differing opinions on the sequence of events; suspect height, description, and physical features. During times of duress, your body is looking to survive, and not looking to lay down accurate memories.

Eyewitnesses can even get male and female confused, or whether a person was young or old. If they can get those seemingly obvious things wrong, then it stands to reason that the smaller details may be wrong too. Why do you think there are those colored markers on the insides of doors, at the bank or store or gas station? That is for the eyewitnesses to estimate the height of a suspect.

I don't know about other police, but I don't usually sit around watching fake cop drama serials on TV, as I have seen enough of that stuff at work. Now, true crime is a different matter altogether. I could literally sit and watch the crime channel 24/7. I love crime, I find it extremely interesting as to why people commit crimes, and I love how all the tiniest pieces come together to solve it.

But, I have never taken crime scene photos home, stuck them on the wall and agonized over them all night, while drinking a glass of wine. Another Hollywoodism. Oh, and one more thing, don't tell your kids that if they are naughty, the police will take them away. Kids should be taught that police are there to help and protect them.

Biggest Pet Peeve

The last thing you want is for a child to have the misconception that police are bad and scary. There may come a time when a child might need to approach a police officer for help, so it shouldn't be a negative experience.

Common Questions

Aside from the myths and misconceptions around policing, there are many common questions that get asked of police. If I had a dollar for every time I have been asked these and other questions like these, I would be living in retirement on a tropical island. Here are some of my all-time faves, that most cops would have been asked too, and my usual answers:

- "Have you shot anyone?" Not today. "Ever?" No.
- "Have you ever punched anyone?" Ah, yep, many times.
- "Has anyone ever punched you?" Yes, but they usually come off second best.
- "Can I see your gun and handcuffs?" Hell no.
- "You are too nice to be a cop." You don't know me.
- "You *don't* look like a cop." You're too kind.
- "You *do* look like a cop." What does a cop look like?
- "Is being a cop like what you see on TV?" Fuck no (age appropriate).
- "Do cops really like donuts and coffee?" Yeah, but not because I'm a cop, asshole.
- "Wanna see me naked?" I would rather scratch my eyes out with a pencil.

- "You are a big tough bitch." Am I? Thanks for letting me know.
- "Can police still arrest a person if they are off duty?" Absolutely.
- "What is the worst thing you have ever seen?" How much time do you have?
- "Would you let your kid be a cop?" Nobody could have talked *me* out of it.
- "Have you ever seen a corrupt cop?" Yes, but luckily those assholes are a minority.
- "Have you ever been offered a bribe?" We all have.
- "Have you ever taken a bribe?" Fuck off, idiot.

But what about when it is not all fun and games, like real crime and crime scenes? Piecing together a crime scene is like putting together a jigsaw puzzle. It may take a while to have all the pieces fit together, but unlike people, physical evidence doesn't lie. Read on to immerse yourself into a crime scene, where blood, guts, and horror awaits.

CHAPTER EIGHT

Evidence And Crime Scenes

When a crime occurs, police attend, and at times, have to establish a crime scene. A crime scene is like a snapshot of a moment frozen in time. Some scenes are horrific and obvious, whilst others can appear more subtle. There are certain procedures that need to be followed to preserve evidence, and ensure anything collected is handled correctly. Jeopardize the evidence and you could jeopardize your whole case.

Crime scenes can tell alot about the crime and the perpetrator, from blood spatter patterns to a person's modus operandi (known as an MO), which literally means their method of operation. Police need to be right on their game—especially with crimes of violence—and it is important to look at scenes with eyes wide open, and figure out if what you are seeing is the truth or a fabrication.

What is a Crime Scene?

Any place that is associated with the commission of a crime is a crime scene. Physical evidence will likely be present and collected by investigators. But the crime scene is not necessarily only where the actual crime occurred. It can encompass vehicles, storage sheds, or any other place that may contain physical evidence linked to that crime.

For example, if a person goes missing, police might search their home and find blood evidence of a crime, then find the vehicle abandoned in a carpark, before finding the body in the woods. Technically, all three locations—the home, the vehicle, and the woods are all a crime scene.

But what if it is an obvious accident? Well, firstly, you need to be sure of what you are looking at. Even if you attend a location, and could determine that it was an accident, it is still treated like a crime scene, where evidence is still collected, photographs and witness statements are still taken.

Imagine that police are called to someone's home, after neighbors called in a disturbance. Upon arrival, the police find a guy that is unconscious, and has blood coming out his head, with a bloodied baseball bat beside him on the ground. There is a female there stating that they were playing around, and it was just an accident. Well, was it?

She says she was swinging the bat, and he came around the corner and she hit him by mistake. Obviously, we can't take her word for it—that she was air-swinging and collided with his head while horsing around. Paramedics arrive and he gets taken to the hospital. Now, remembering that people bullshit all the time, you must still treat the area as a crime scene unless you discover evidence to the contrary.

You would obviously photograph the scene, take the bat into evidence, and take a statement from the woman. Lucky for her, he woke up in the hospital and when asked what happened, he said that his sister was practising her swing in the living room, and he jumped out to scare her. She was startled and nearly took his head off.

Now, if he woke up and said she had threatened to kill him and was chasing him around the house with a baseball bat, then we would be glad we collected that evidence so that charges could be laid.

Establishing a Crime Scene

When a crime has occurred, it is critical to obtain crime scene evidence as soon as possible. Any delays in obtaining evidence can result in contamination of the scene, people getting rid of evidence, or the reduction in quality of potential samples. It is imperative to establish your crime scene which may include creating a perimeter, using crime scene tape, or having a command post and officers guarding the scene.

This, of course, all depends on the severity of the crime, but is certainly the case with crimes involving violence. The perimeter may be visual with barricades, or police tape to seal off the location, or it may not be so defined, with patrol units strategically placed around a scene. A command post is essential in major or ongoing crimes, such as a siege or hostage situation, a major traffic accident, or ongoing natural disaster.

It's like having a mini police station right at the site of the incident. But again, a command post does not have to be a physical building, it could be senior officers utilizing a vehicle or other designated area to conduct operations and planning.

When attending a crime scene, it is very important to keep an open mind, and take all possible scenarios into account. Police cannot be too quick to find a resolution, as they may miss crucial evidence of the crime. Look for what *is* there, anything obviously out of the ordinary—such as any weapons left behind, anything that shouldn't be there or stands out.

I have been to many home break-and-enter incidents where the suspect inadvertently leaves an item behind—like, you know, his wallet. Has the missing victim left her pocket-book and phone behind? Is that normal behavior for that person? Equally as important, but often overlooked, is ascertaining what is *not* there.

Are there items missing from the home? Has the victim's wallet or jewelry been taken? Are there weapons missing from the gun cabinet? Many a criminal mind has tried to outsmart police, and as I mentioned previously, it is not necessarily the police, but the evidence that trips them up.

Staging a Scene

Since the dawn of time, people have staged crime scenes to conceal a crime, throw police off track, minimize their involvement, or protect a loved one. Staging a crime scene involves tampering with evidence and altering the "appearance" of the crime to be something else. I once attended an apparent suicide by hanging of a member of an outlaw motorcycle gang.

He was hanging by the neck from a metal beam in his garage after "stepping off" a chair. Looked pretty standard, with the chair tipped over, his eyes were bulging, and his jacket had slipped down off his shoulders and down his arms, probably because he was struggling to breathe. But what started as a routine suicide, ended up being a murder.

As officers searched the body for identification—and, in the process, moved the jacket around—they discovered his hands tied together. Upon lifting his shirt to check for other injuries, they discovered he was battered and bruised all over the torso. Scene staged.

Common Themes

Police see lots of crime scenes, and you do start to develop a sense of when something is not quite right. Of course, there are always exceptions to any rule, but there are also many commonalities between crime scenes, so if a cop has a gut feeling that something is off, it likely is.

For instance, it is very rare for a female to commit suicide naked, or for a female to shoot themselves in the face. Why, you ask? Well, because of the inherent nature of women as nurturers. A woman who wanted to kill herself would likely not do it naked, because believe it or not, she would be worried about paramedics and police seeing her naked—yes, even after she is dead.

If a woman wants to commit suicide, pills are a preferred method. A woman shooting herself does happen, but is not that common. But if a woman did shoot herself, it is generally not in the face, as again they don't want to destroy their faces, or cause a mess for the family. This is not always the case every time, but it is usual.

Women can still be quite considerate in suicide and will mostly avoid leaving in a violent manner. Again, there are exceptions, where I have seen women jump off buildings, and in front of trains, and they were obviously not worried about making a mess.

Crime scenes can be dirty, smelly, bloody, and downright horrific. When there is evidence of trauma to a person, it can be quite confronting. As outlined before, death has a very significant smell to it, but so does blood.

When you attend a scene that has a large amount of blood, there is a distinct metal-like smell, due to its iron content. Crime scenes can contain blood, body fluids, body parts, pieces of brain, entrails, and other types of matter.

Crime scenes can get into your head if you let them, so I always told younger officers to go take a look, satisfy your curiosity, collect your evidence, and get out of there if possible. If you don't need to be standing over a body for long amounts of time, then don't. Trust me, they all build up on you.

Forensic and Physical Evidence

Forensic evidence is that which is collected using scientific methods—the results of which can be used in court proceedings, and can include such things as DNA tests, blood typing, and ballistic testing. Physical evidence is any tangible item, material, or object gathered at a crime scene, and relevant to the case for use in criminal proceedings—such as a murder weapon, clothing or footprints.

There are many ways in which physical evidence can build a picture of how a crime occurred. Again, physical evidence doesn't lie—if presented and processed correctly. There are many types of evidence collected at crime scenes, which can then be photographed, fingerprinted, or samples collected and sent to a laboratory for further testing.

Blood is obviously a major piece of evidence in any crime scene, and can tell many things such as blood type, DNA, or the presence of any toxic substances in the body. But apart from lab tests, blood patterns can be very telling pieces of evidence.

Blood Spatter

The way in which blood leaves the body—and is distributed at a crime scene—can indicate many things. Blood spatter analysis studies the way in which blood is affected by gravity and motion, after exiting the body. Blood has cohesive properties which causes it to group together and create patterns.

For example, blood dripping slowly from a weapon will drop vertically and produce round droplets, if someone is standing still. If that person is moving—say walking or running— then the droplets spread and change shape when coming into contact with a surface. The shape of a blood stain can tell alot about the direction the blood came from.

As mentioned, if a blood droplet fell vertically, it would still be somewhat round, whereas blood traveling at speed or an angle, will cause a more elongated pattern. There are many methods of measurement to determine the angle that a blood droplet has traveled, which may help to piece the scene together.

But there are many other considerations when analyzing blood spatter, such as the contact surface. Rough and smooth contact surfaces can alter the shape and size of the droplet. Low velocity spatter, from a low impact injury, will usually produce blood drips. Medium velocity spatter—maybe from a knife wound—can produce spurting of blood. High velocity spatter is the type you would see from a gunshot wound and can be more mist or spray like.

Another type of spatter is cast off, which generally occurs when a weapon is used, such as the use of a baseball bat to strike a victim repeatedly, where blood is cast off the bat onto the ceiling or wall with every backswing.

Gunshot Residue

Gunshot residue is another telling piece of physical evidence, when a firearm is used in the commission of a crime. When a person discharges a firearm, is in close proximity to someone who has fired a gun, or touches a recently fired gun, residue will transfer to the person's hands, skin, and clothing. Gunshot residue (or GSR) is made up of gunpowder, particles of the shell casing, the primer cap of the round, and any other propellant.

When a person pulls the trigger of a gun, the firing pin will come into contact with the primer cap of the ammunition and cause a mini-explosion and flames. This causes an ignition of the gunpowder, and the high pressure and temperature then expels the bullet from the gun. If you have ever seen a firearm shot in darkness, you will be familiar with this muzzle flash.

Remember that guy a few chapters back that shot himself in the head while on the phone with his estranged wife? Well, this is an example of where the evidence proved to the medical examiner that this death was, in fact, a suicide by shooting.

The victim had a large amount of GSR on his forehead and hands. As for those weird muscle contractions I spoke about upon death, his finger had spasmed and was still bent on the trigger, so it was determined that it could not have possibly been staged.

Photographs

Photographs are another method police use to capture evidence in-situ, which is a Latin phrase meaning "in position" or "in place." Photographic evidence is critical to court proceedings, and crime scene photographs are notoriously graphic and can be disturbing to look at. There is no editing, there is no sugar coating, just the raw, plain, honest truth.

Surprisingly, a victim's family members may request to see the crime scene photos. Of course, it is not something that is encouraged as it can be extremely distressing, but some people just need that extra proof and they have that right. Some families want to see the crime scene photos with their own eyes, to gain an understanding of what happened to their loved one.

I went to a workplace accident where a male forklift operator had run over a female co-worker. It was investigated thoroughly, and was determined an accident. The scene was particularly gruesome, as the forklift had run into her, knocked her down, and completely run over her.

She was bent and twisted in all positions, she was ripped open, exposing yellow fatty tissue, blood everywhere, and her guts were blown out through her ass. Horrific and totally senseless accident. The driver had his forklift loaded up so high he could not see where he was going, so he reversed down a laneway and into a car space, to then drive forward where he was going to peek through the load.

As he reversed, his co-worker had exited the factory through a nearby doorway for a bath-room break. He didn't see her and ran her down. I remember attending the coroner's court matter, and the mother demanded to see the crime scene photos. At first, I refused and tried to gently explain the graphic nature of the pics, but she insisted that she had to see with her own eyes.

It felt so wrong, but I showed her because I realized it was not about me. Remember that bad car accident, with the teenager that was dying, and his buddy was dead in the passenger seat? That poor father of the teen that died would call me every day, and ask me the same question. He would ask me if his son was wearing a seatbelt when he died.

I tried to assure him every day that he was, but he would ring the next day and ask again. This went on for a few weeks and, of course, I did not mind trying to reassure him. After a few weeks, he finally asked me how I knew for sure that his son had been wearing the seatbelt. I mean, I had told him every day that I had seen it with my own eyes, and that he was clutching the seatbelt upon impact.

He wanted more proof, so I gently told him that his son had a large bruise in a line all the way across his chest, which we had discovered at the autopsy. He also wanted to see the photographs of the bruise, so I eventually showed him. This might sound like a cold and weird thing to do, but it completely put his and his wife's minds at ease.

These grieving parents now had confirmation that their son was doing the right thing. It is exactly what they needed. It is not for me to judge or control what people need, to make peace with the death of their loved ones. Like I said before, it was not about me. And the phone calls stopped.

Crime scenes can be tricky little buggers to navigate, as there is so much going on, but it is critical to the case to handle and preserve evidence correctly, and establish a crime scene quickly. The quality of the case can depend on how well the crime scene is processed. Done poorly, and the bad guys have a chance at getting away with—sometimes—murder.

Crime scenes speak volumes about what has happened at that point in time, and it is up to officers to look at the finer details and keep their eyes open. Is this what actually happened or what someone wants me to *think* has happened? Crime scenes can be quite heavy to stand around in for any length of time, but it is a necessary part of the job.

Some parts are just plain boring, like guarding a crime scene, but there are other bits of the job that are exciting. Up next is all the good, bad, and boring bits of policing, but trust me, the bad bits are outweighed by the exciting parts, and you won't want to miss this.

CHAPTER NINE

The Good, The Bad, And The Boring

Every minute of every day can be different. Even attending two similar jobs—it's still different. Sure, when you have been a cop for a while, sometimes it can become routine, but the individual officer's attitude to their job can make all the difference.

No two days are the same, which is great for someone like me that gets bored easily. I was under no illusion that policing was all out action and excitement—like in the movies. I knew it was going to be scary, confronting, and gruesome at times, and would be filled with endless paperwork. That is just a given. Policing is rewarding, exciting, diverse, and challenging but there are certainly good, bad, and boring bits.

The Good Bits

So, what is good about policing? Well, I would be lying if I said that I don't like action. I loved the action. I love to be on the move, getting amongst everything, and sorting out problems. I don't fuck around, and I am very straight-forward. I got the job done, and done well.

When confronted with a potential arrest scenario, sometimes you just have to react and go right in. Other times, you basically give the person the chance to determine how this will go down—the easy way or the hard way—and I am happy to do both. One thing is for sure; as a cop, you must come out on top.

You can't back down. You can retreat and get backup, say if you're one out and being shot at, but you can't back down. Imagine going to a bar room brawl, and not taking charge, saying,

"Okay, everyone, let's just calm down" or being told to fuck off and telling them you'll come back later. Not an option.

An exciting part of police work is high-speed vehicle pursuits. You are cruising around town, eating donuts and drinking coffee (insert cheeky cough here), when you get a call from the dispatcher that there has been a bank robbery. The first thing cops will do after responding a definite "yes we will attend" is put the windows of the patrol car up.

Why? Because the next thing would be to turn on the flashing lights and sirens. Sirens are loud enough at any time, worse when you are driving and trying to listen to the police radio. But they are even louder with the windows down. Rookie mistake.

There is something about lights and sirens that gets the adrenaline going—it is undeniable. You are likely driving fast, with all your warning signals activated, talking to the radio dispatcher, you see the suspect vehicle and shit goes off from there. The bad guys see the patrol car, and it's on. High speed pursuit. Now that is exciting.

Foot pursuits are also fun, although not as much as chasing someone in a car. Sometimes when dealing with suspects they will run for no reason—at unexpected times. Just when you think everything is under control, they bolt. Chasing someone on foot is alot more work.

For a start, you have to run, and chase them, jump fences, run through backyards, dodge pets and dogs, and then if you do catch up, you have to maybe crash-tackle them and cuff them up. Now you can see why I bang on about fitness. You really owe it yourself to be in good physical condition.

This next bit might sound strange, but another cool part of the job is when you have to break into houses or cars to assist someone. I have had to smash car windows with a baton to help kids trapped in a hot car. It looks easy, we have all seen it done on TV, but holy shit, it is hard. You have to hit a window at a decent angle or the baton will just keep bouncing back off it.

I have had to break into houses before, too, by opening or smashing windows and climbing in to look for someone that hasn't been seen for days, or an old person who has taken a fall. Sometimes I have had to kick doors in to get access, which is not always as easy as it looks. Remember stinky puffed up blowfly man? Well, we tried to kick that door in, but it was near impossible to get enough leverage, as the top step was very narrow, so we chopped it down.

Training is something I loved as well. Not training in the classroom, reading countless books, and debating the universe—I am talking about real training. Weapons training. I loved weapons training so much that I almost became a weapons instructor, which would have made me one of two female weapons instructors at the time (in a force of 15,000 officers).

I went to a weapons training day with my fellow local officers, and I was stripping down my Glock 9mm semi-automatic pistol and rebuilding it in record time. I kicked the ass of all the guys, and yes, I was trying to, as I'm competitive. The instructor asked me if I wanted to do the weapons trainer course, and I jumped at the chance.

The course was to be completed at the police academy and would have been a few weeks away at a time. I did have three kids under three years old by then, but was still super keen to go. I was majorly disappointed when the course was canceled due to funding at the time, and a lack of numbers. I didn't get the opportunity again, as I had moved on by then.

Other police tools of the trade include the baton, taser, pepper spray, and handcuffs. Unfortunately, I had left the force right before tasers came in, so I never got the pleasure of using it, but I certainly got well-trained in the use of pepper spray. When pepper spray became available to our department, a part of being trained in the use of it was to have it wiped all over your face, then water was sprayed on it, which activated it quickly.

I was pissed and I told my husband that I was not doing that. He had been to the training that day and had to go through it. I was adamant that this was bullshit and I was not doing it. I went to the training, dug my toes in and told the instructor that I didn't need to get shot by a gun to know it fucking hurts, so why would I need to get sprayed?

He must have felt I had a point and he let me off without having to do it. *Well, fuck me.* The karma bus hit me about a week later, when I was out on a job and my partner (you know who you are) went to spray a suspect I was arresting, and fucking hit me instead. Worst pain ever. It just burns and burns and burns…

Arrests can be fun, dangerous and risky, but fun. Some people don't like getting down and dirty with suspects, but it's your job. Luckily, it doesn't bother me, and I actually enjoyed it. Policing can take you to places that the average person doesn't go, and sometimes you meet people that you wouldn't normally meet.

It is common to provide guard duties for politicians, celebrities, prominent sports figures, and attend concerts, shows, and major sporting events. One of the inner-city stations I worked at, where I met my husband, was right near a large concert venue and we would have to go and help with crowd control. It was great, and I saw nearly every international singer or band that performed there for the three years I was there. Better than buying tickets.

The Bad Bits

With the good comes the bad. It is unavoidable and a reality, but as long as the good outweighs the bad then you are still in front. Shift work sucks. It is just not normal to be up all hours of the night, and trying to sleep all day. We are not nocturnal, we are not owls, we are meant to sleep at night. Did I mention shift work sucks?

When I first joined the force, we would work eight-hour shifts with the worst starting at eleven o'clock at night and finishing at seven o'clock in the morning, for one week straight. You would just start to get used to the hours, and then have five days off, and back to the day shift. Sleeping during the day sucks too.

I would get a few winks here and there but found it very hard to get sound sleep, especially with three kids in the house. Later, in an effort to reduce overtime, they changed the shifts to twelve hours. The theory was that if the outgoing shift got an arrest close to knock-off time, that the oncoming shift would take it.

Didn't happen that way when the oncoming shift had their own urgent jobs to get to, so some days were upward of sixteen hours. Not cool. Shift work also takes you away from family, and friends, and makes it hard to commit to social functions, because you can bet your ass you are likely going to be working when they are on.

Police work is downright dangerous. You could head out to work and never come home, which is true of any job, but the odds are much higher in this particular line of work. The nature of the job puts you in contact with unpredictable, drug affected, and armed suspects on a daily basis, which elevates your chances of getting killed or injured. There is the risk of death at every call, and that is not being dramatic, it is being realistic.

I have known plenty of cops that have gone to a routine domestic violence call, which turned deadly very fast. I have known officers that have been killed in car accidents on duty, and others that have been shot and killed by suspects trying to avoid capture. It happens. And when it does, it ripples through the department like a tidal wave. I think it's because we all know, at any time, it could be us.

The job is gruesome at times, with horrific sights that cannot be unseen. There is blood, trauma, missing body parts, heads separated from bodies, deceased children, and autopsies. This is the shitty part of the job, especially when an innocent person gets caught up in someone else's tragedy.

When a scumbag gets blown away, or a drug dealer gets popped, you can justify that in your mind, and probably even feel that they deserved it because of their lifestyle. But when an elderly person is bashed to death in their home, or a young girl is abducted and murdered, you can't help but feel for them, and unfortunately, sometimes relate that to your own family.

Death messages are no better, and are hard to deliver at any time, but especially when you know the family. Death is a big part of the job that you have to be prepared for. You do get used to it to a degree, but I hate being reminded that we do actually die one day.

The job can also be dirty when rolling around on the ground wrestling suspects, or pulling drug crops. It can be hazardous to your health when you are dealing with injured or diseased people, or standing in the rain doing traffic duty for hours, without a raincoat (yes that happened to me). *So* shit.

The Boring Bits

With the good naturally comes the bad, but the boring is neither good or bad, it's just boring. It is not high-speed pursuits, gun battles, and action all the time. There is downtime too. Some tasks are notoriously boring, not so much because of the crime itself, but mostly due to the waiting.

For example, no cop likes to sit around the court house all day waiting to give evidence, only to be told you are not going to get on the stand that day after all. Guarding crime scenes is boring because even though the crime might have been pretty wild, it sucks to have to sit in a patrol car, usually on your own, and make sure nobody enters.

Guarding suspects in hospitals is another boring part of the job. If a suspect is injured during the commission of a crime and needs to go to hospital, as police have a duty of care, then you better be prepared to sit around for hours and wait.

Hostage and siege situations can be really fucking boring too, as there is a lot of negotiating going on behind the scenes, but you may not be a part of that, and may be stuck out on an outer perimeter. Waiting.

Surveillance is the same. You could sit in a car all night, and watch a house and see fuck all. It is not like in the movies where they sit and wait about five minutes, and the guy rocks up home. Nightshift can be a drag if it is a quiet night, and you have pulled station duty. It sucks when you are stuck inside, everyone is out all night, and you are there alone with nothing to do.

But the most boring job of all, in my opinion, is paperwork. You have shitloads of paperwork, especially if you have matters going to court. If you are not good with paperwork, and details, it is a very painful process.

But it's all in the attitude. Expect there to be some shitty days, and then you are not dis-illusioned when they come around. I knew I was stepping into a world where I would have to face scary and confronting scenes and people, but it is what it is. Policing is still the best job I have ever had, and I have struggled to find something as rewarding and challenging since.

Police work is one big life lesson, and I am about to share with you what I learned about life from being a cop. I know that you will be able to implement these into your own life, regardless of who you are. You don't need to be a cop to benefit from these, so let's take a look now.

CHAPTER TEN

Life Lessons From Law Enforcement

It's not possible to spend fifteen years as a cop, dealing with life, death, tragedy, crime, and everything in between and not be affected in some way. I am eternally grateful for my time as a cop, and I strongly encourage others to do the same. I would never talk someone out of their dream, as that is not my place.

Women can be cops, and I have learned so many lessons that I am going to share with you. These lessons are not strictly for people wanting to be cops, they are just things I learned about life from being a cop that you can also use in your own life. If there is just one of my life lessons, or just one little thing that resonates with you, then this has all been worth it.

My life in law enforcement was good, bad, and at times ugly, but I absolutely loved my job. I didn't grow up wanting to be a cop, but when I decided to do it, nothing was going to stop me. People tried to influence me by saying it was dangerous and I could get killed. Yep, and I could walk out the front door and get hit by a bus.

It's a sad reality that people get killed every day at work, cops or not. I was a cop since the age of twenty, but after a husband, three kids and fifteen years' service, I had come to the end of my policing road. When I joined the force, I promised myself that if I ever found that I had had enough of it, I would leave gracefully and not hang around to become bitter and twisted.

So, after wrestling bad guys for fifteen years, I felt that I had gotten all that I wanted to get out of it, and the time had come to move on to new things. Jason had left the force a few months before me, and I saw him out in civilian life—

loving it—and thought to myself, "What am I still doing here?" It was a hard decision to leave the force after so long, as I had spent most of my adult life as a cop.

I don't regret leaving when I did, it was the best thing to do at the time. My three sons were still only very young, and I was happy to put all my energy into them. I would be lying if I said I don't miss it—I do. Well, I don't miss shift work, dead bodies, and courtwork, but I miss *being* a cop at times.

It was a big part of my life and I loved almost every minute. But even though I am no longer a cop, I still live by the life lessons that I took from policing and transferred into everyday life. When you have done a job like that for as long as I did, and from an early age, it gets imprinted into your very being—it becomes who you are.

I couldn't *not* act like a cop if I tried. I still keep my eyes wide open, will argue my point when I need to, and I never back down from anyone. Neither should you. It is not possible to have been a cop for as long as I was, and be naïve enough to think that I didn't learn anything about life from it.

There is something about seeing people at their worst that really opens your eyes, and your mind, to how people live and what troubles they have in their lives. A police officer sees all facets of human nature, and sometimes there is good stuff, but people usually only call us when things are not going well. Tragedy, injury, emergency, death, or crime is the normal reason for the call.

So, here is what I learned and continue to live by today, and maybe you might get something from my life lessons too, regardless of who you are, where you work, or what you do. You don't need to be a cop to get some benefit out of these, and they can apply to anybody in any situation.

Maybe some of this was in my genetic makeup already, my mom was a bit of a spitfire too, but either way, the police force shaped me into the person I am today, and I am forever grateful for the time I spent there. I experienced things I never would have if I didn't join. It opened my eyes up to the world and I was able to see how the other half lives.

Remember, I came from a very small lakeside town where everybody knows the name of everybody's dog. There were many ups, some downs, and some things lie in between, but I don't regret it for a moment. I still miss it at times and would do it all again in a heartbeat. Here are some life lessons I learned from being a police officer and I hope you can take something away from them. Even just one thing.

Life Lessons Learned From Law Enforcement

- Don't let anybody, even family, talk you out of your dreams. When I decided to become a cop, nobody could have talked me out of it if they tried. Some people were supportive, others were not, and I did not let that affect me. Don't be afraid to be different, and go against the flow.
- Once you achieve your dream and reach your goals, don't let others negatively influence

you. I was so excited to be a cop, and when I got to my first station, there were so many jaded cops that should have left long ago. Don't let people piss on your rainbow.

- If you don't like where you are in your job right now, change it. "Yeah but I can't." Yes, you can. There is always an option. Remember my shitty bank job? Didn't like it, changed it. Even a small micro-change is a change. Just do it (sorry, Nike).

- You know what your dreams are. If you don't have a dream, get one. It doesn't need to be huge, it doesn't need to be profound or philosophical. It's yours. I wanted to be a cop, people asked why, expecting a powerful answer, and I said I joined because I wanted to—and that is the truth. Set goals. And when you get there, set a new one.

- When you get close enough to your dream that you can smell it, fear will likely raise its fucking ugly head. Don't be afraid. When I went to the academy and waved goodbye to my mom from the train, I panicked and thought, *What the fuck am I doing?* Then I said to myself, "I chose this." Be careful what you wish for because good things will come your way.

- Stand up for your principles, and for those around you. If you see someone being hardly done by, say something about it. If you are being wronged, stand up for yourself. Nobody has the right to cut you down. Wake up, kick ass, repeat.

- Don't be afraid to take a chance on something new, and don't let fear of the unknown stop you from achieving your dreams. Create some micro goals and some new "firsts" for yourself. Some of my first experiences in the job were daunting but the best part about your first "whatever" is that you only need to do it once. After that, technically, you have experience.

- Life is unpredictable, just like police work, and we never know what the day will bring. Embrace what you can, let go of what you don't need, and face what you must. Be present and show up every day.

- Keep an open mind about everything in this world. Don't believe everything you see on the news, in the papers, or even what people tell you. People lie for their own gain. Be smart—be in front of that game. Be curious and suspicious. You call the shots.

- When you encounter someone having a shitty day, or they are rude, or obnoxious— try not to take it personally. We never know what is going on in someone's life and they may have been a model citizen right up until you cross paths. Try not to be dragged into someone else's shit. Ever.

- When people do all sorts of crazy shit, you can't control how they act, but you can control how *you* react. I remember when I used to train junior police officers and they would react badly to an angry person, and get all flustered. I would say, "Don't let anybody raise your blood pressure."

- Situations and people are not always as they seem, just like a crime scene, you need to have your eyes open to what is around you. Keep your wits about you, and know your surroundings. Trust your instincts, if you feel something is off, it probably is. Listen to that.

- When you get confronted with death, and you will at some stage, try to keep it in perspective, that it was that person's journey, and it's not about you. This might sound harsh, but it will help you protect yourself.

- Death is the great leveler and restores equality to us all. Don't be afraid to live your life to the fullest. When it is your time, death will be ready, and it will find you wherever you are, so you might as well live fearlessly until then.

- Clean undies are not crucial, as they will get messed up anyway if you die. Not very profound, just seeing if you are still paying attention (hahaha).

- Nobody can change the world, not even you, but that doesn't mean you don't try. It just means you don't need to turn yourself inside out trying to make a difference. It might seem noble to say you want to change the world, but be realistic and break it down into bite-size chunks. Do some good every day.

- Whatever job you do, do it well, and make a positive impact on the person you are dealing with. In the bank, one of my wise, older work-mates gave me some sage advice, that I still use today. When it was busy and I would get nervous that people were lined up out the door, she would say to me, "You can only serve the person that is standing in front of you."

- You are your number one asset, and you need to protect yourself at all times. Protect yourself physically by getting a little fitter, or maybe learning some self defense. Protect yourself emotionally, too, by being careful who you give your time, energy, and power to, regardless of who they are. Don't give 100% to everybody else, keep some for yourself.

- Humor is a great defense as a cop, and making light of a situation is a coping mechanism. You see some fucking awful shit that can't be unseen. You can use this too in everyday life, I know I do. Not just to combat bad shit, but laughing just for the sake of laughing. Laugh hard and laugh often.

- Never feel that you are at a disadvantage for being female. I worked in a male-dominated profession, and I brought certain perspectives and qualities to the job. Guys have qualities that we may or may not have, but don't let anybody ever make you feel that you are less of a person by being a woman, or a man for that matter.

- You can have marriage, kids, and a career even with shift work. It is not easy but it is possible to do it. Don't let that stop you from having your dream job. You are resourceful and smart, just get it done.

- Stress can be a part of a police officer's life due to the nature of the job, but it can be a major part of anybody's life. Don't let stress rule you, you must take control of it, and knock it on the head, or it will kill you. You need to find things that combat your stress, and remind yourself to actively take that time.

- Some people have zero regard, or respect for the people around them. Steer clear and don't let others drag you down with them. Cut away bad influences or negativity from others, and don't let them weigh you down.

- Don't let anybody push you around. If you find people are trying to punk you, set boundaries, and teach them what you will accept and when they are crossing the line. You can't expect people to read your mind and know what will piss you off. If something or someone does, tell them. One of my favorite things to say is, "if I'm thinking it, you'll know about it."

- Don't take shit from anybody, at all, ever. I told my boys this from a very early age. This does not mean that you go ballistic on people that piss you off, it just means that you stand up for yourself. You can do that in an assertive, non-threatening way. Stand up for you—you're important and worth it. You are nobody's bitch.

So, there you have it. This book is me on a page. It has been one hell of a journey, and a wild ride, and I hope you can take some tips and make them your own.

You are amazing, so be strong, be awesome, and bring it every day.

To those that are in law enforcement or considering it: be bold, be brave, you got this.

Lethal

ACKNOWLEDGMENTS

To the New South Wales Police Force, thanks for the experiences that made this possible.

To my coach, author Lise Cartwright, for keeping me sane, thank you is not enough.

To my editors, Qat Wanders and Christy Leos, thanks for getting this book to make sense.

To Danijela Mijailovic for the killer cover, interior design and making sure it all looks good.

To Self-Publishing School, thanks for showing me the way.

To my Launch Team, a massive thanks to those who helped to get this book out there. You helped me more than you know, and it means the world to me to have you involved:

Lisa Andersen, Heather Armstrong, Melanie Avery, Shane Black, Janice Boyd, Janice Cahill,

Aza Clave, Lisa Cook, Katy Crofts, Gillian Duncan, Vanessa Ellis, Kathy Flora, Jaki Gore, Tom Gose, JC Graham, Rhonda Hazey, Wendy Huish, Esther Louis Jacques, Annie Kenniff, Michaela Kenniff, Lindsay Kuehster, Jackie Lamb, Donna Loftus, Jackie McCarthy, Michelle McCulloch, Julz McGrath, Rachael McMahon, Michelle Matthews, Kristy Messer, Peter Moore, Mary Morrison, Wendy Munro, Mark Munro, Ashley Nehez, Janice Nehez, Stephen Nehez, Jr., Kelly Nicholls, Sarah Paulson, Stefeny Pyle, Carol Richardson, Jaime Richardson, Monica Rubombora, Leena St Michael, Caryl Saunders-King, Jessie Simonas, Kathie Smith, Selena Smith, Judson Somerville, Brooke Tarr, Melinda Threlkeld, Annette Tutton, Carlah Walton, Carmel Ward, John Weiler, Dee Wiggins and Nandita Yadav.

SELF-PUBLISHING
SCHOOL

NOW IT'S YOUR TURN

**Discover the EXACT 3-step blueprint
you need to become a bestselling
author in 3 months.**

Self-Publishing School helped me,
and now I want them to help you with this
FREE WEBINAR!

Even if you're busy, bad at writing,
or don't know where to start, you CAN
write a bestseller and build your best life.

With tools and experience across a variety
niches and professions, Self-Publishing School
is the <u>only</u> resource you need to take
your book to the finish line!

DON'T WAIT

Watch this FREE WEBINAR now, and
Say "YES" to becoming a bestseller:

https://xe172.isrefer.com/go/
sps4fta-vts/bookbrosinc6744

ABOUT THE AUTHOR

Lisa Doble is an Australian ex-cop, wife, mother and author. She spent fifteen years in the New South Wales Police Force and patrolled the streets in various country and metropolitan locations.

Lisa completed a Bachelor of Social Science, majoring in Counter-Terrorism, Criminology & Forensic Science. She still maintains a strong interest in those topics.

Lisa has published articles in the Australian Police Journal on terrorism topics, including the rise of Foreign Fighters, Radicalization and Violent Extremism.

She has experience in recruitment, where she sought high performing executives for companies within the Guns and Ammunition industry, in the United States.

Lisa had a lifelong dream to write a book and has had that passion since childhood.

When she was about 8 years old, she wrote a book full of poems and short stories and decided at that age, that she would one day publish it. She lost the book....

Over recent years Lisa has worked in the field of child protection, working in the investigation and assessment team. She has also been conducting family conferencing, both in the government and private sector.

When Lisa is not on the back of a horse, at the gym, or trail running, she is walking the dog, drinking coffee and writing more books.

If you would like to get in touch, Lisa can be found on all forms of social media, or email
lisadoble@hotmail.com

Firstly, thank you for reading and making it
this far. Your support is appreciated.

As a self-published author,
I rely on reviews like yours.

If you loved the book or learned some
new stuff, I would be forever grateful
if you could leave your honest review
on the Amazon page.

This will help more people, like you,
to find my book.

Again, thank you so much for the support,
until next time....

Lisa Doble

Made in the USA
Middletown, DE
06 November 2019